a practical guide to

INTIMACY in MARRIAGE

Costa Mitchell

ISBN 978-0-6397-2546-8

First published 1990

2nd Edition 1991

3rd Edition 2000, Vineyard International Publishing

4th Edition 2002, Vineyard International Publishing

5th Edition 2022, Self-published Illustrations copyright © 2022 by Candy Preston Cover design by Candy Preston

Foreword

I met Jesus Christ in August 1982 and my life changed. Spiritual regeneration opened my eyes and brought a new perspective on life and its challenges. In particular, I was challenged about my role as a husband and as the head of my family. Whether we like it or not, we need to be challenged about our marriages because the success of this relationship is foundational to our happiness.

I was intrigued by the observation of a marriage guidance counsellor that most couples do not love one another- they do not even particularly like each other - but are kept together by the fear of loneliness and financial necessity. Unrealistic expectations of marriage cause men and women to look elsewhere for fulfilment. The expert blamed television and soap operas for encouraging these false ideals and impossible fantasies.

What hope is there for marriage then? I would have thrown up my hands in despair had I not realized that marriage is an institution ordained by God. And marriage, like everything else in the Christian life, has to be worked at. God made men and women different to fulfil their special roles in loving each other. Instead of decrying the differences and trying to negate them, we need to recognize them and met Jesus Christ in August 1982 and my life and allow God to use them to strengthen the marriage bond. Marriage is high on God's list of priorities. It comes before business, sport, hobbies or recreation and requires 100 percent effort from both partners. The marriage relationship is used to represent the union of Christ with his people. Such is its importance. God therefore intends this relationship to be a meaningful one.

God has laid down important ground rules for marriage. Communication and an unselfish accommodation of each other are essential. Costa's readable, practical guide addresses the ongoing challenge of marriage. It is written with the conviction that unfulfilling marriages can be restored to their full potential. I pray that, for all who read it, this book will be the catalyst for the enjoyment of one of God's greatest gifts - a fulfilling marriage.

Bless you all.

Peter Pollock

Introduction

No this is not a sex manual! Yes, it is about how to make your sex life more meaningful, and more. It is about preventing at least two of the top three causes of divorce from occurring in your marriage: the chief complaint of women - poor or not enough communication, and of men -poor or not enough sex. More importantly, it is about restoring to every aspect of married life the real meaning of the often used but seldom understood word - "love".

You and I are Purpose-built! We are not an accidental chromosome stew in motion, but rather we have been intricately designed and created, and the Creator has left an imprint - fingerprints in the clay of the unique sculpture that is you. Happiness is the by-product of discovering that purpose, in any area of life, and stress, sadness and disaster are the result of applying the product to the wrong purpose (think of an electric lawnmower being used to clean the swimming pool!)

The purpose of marriage is to bring about oneness, unity or communion between two people. The single Bible verse that tells us this (repeated at least 3, if not 4 times, throughout the Bible) is genesis 2:24 which reads, in the New Living Translation: "...a man (will) leave his father and mother and is joined to his wife, and the two are united into one."

I believe that this purpose and its manifestation as a desire for intimacy is built into humans as part of our genetic code. When a married person does not experience the fulfilment of this drive to oneness, the result is disillusionment or a loss of meaning. I believe that marriage is meant to be a satisfying, growing, growth-producing relationship, from the wedding day, "till death us do part". The initial honeymoon should never end, but instead should lead to many honeymoons in an improving and never-ending cycle. The fact that this is not the experience of a great many couples, and that the Western world is seeing so many marriages ending in divorce, or the complete replacement of marriage by the easy-come, easy-go model of cohabitation without commitment, has a great deal to do with poor modelling and a lack of education about marriage.

When we talk about education in an area like intimacy, many people react defensively. I am aware of the difficulties raised by the idea that we have to teach people how to have intimacy. However, many authors and social scientists will agree that "love is a skill that can be learned". I am convinced, after many years of counselling in this area, that most of the difficulties in marriage relationships can be overcome by a combination of attitude correction and skills training. I have proved to myself and to many doubters that good marriage partners - as is the case with good managers, good sales people and good communicators on all fronts - are made, not born.

I remember a favourite "Peanuts" cartoon that illustrates the point, in which Charlie Brown is walking home dejectedly, baseball bat over his shoulder. He mutters to himself: "A hundred and forty-three to nothing! How could we lose like that when we were so sincere!" The fact is that, in marriage, baseball, business or driving along a freeway, sincerity is not enough. People have car accidents even though they sincerely do not want to. You can be sincere and yet sincerely wrong about things that can hurt or destroy you and other people.

Our marriages and family lives are failing, not because we want them to or because we are insincere, but because the sexual revolution and the information explosion are not in sync. We have increased expectations of sexual satisfaction or intimacy, but this is coupled with the strange belief that "doing what comes naturally" is enough to guarantee success in marriage and that new information in this field is unimportant. South African males in particular have grown up with the belief that "I'm man enough to know how to handle my own life. I don't need any outsiders to tell me how to live – or love my wife!" - especially when it comes to marriage. Our firm faith in our macho infallibility has led us down a relational cul-de-sac, and when we hit the wall we are unable to admit that we have made a mistake. We back out of the relationship and think that a new partner will solve everything. As one man put it: "When I was about to marry, I had an ideal. It turned into an ordeal. Now I want a new deal!"

In 1621 Robert Burton wrote in *Anatomy of Melancholy*: "One was never married, and that's his hell; another is, and that's his plague". This is the experience of many – not being sure whether it is better to marry or to remain single. Their dissatisfaction is tragic, but very avoidable. Our situation is not changed by altering the environment we live in or our lifestyle. Nor is it helped by opting for the alternative many are choosing, of cohabitation without commitment, "because at least when we have to get out, it won't cost us anything". The end of such relationships is every bit as damaging to the psyche of the participants.

My hope is that this book will provide the means to create a new deal in our marriages before they become an ordeal. And if they have already become an ordeal, to remake them into that new deal. The grass is greener than we have known, but it is on our side of the fence!

Although this book is designed for the ordinary person in the street, or rather, in the home, I have drawn on a number of professional sources, often of the expert variety, while trying to put their expertise in easily digestible form. I have also sought to make this treatment of the subject as exhaustive as is possible in such a short volume.

Chapter 1 lays the foundation for what follows by presenting the need for, the hindrances to and the "how to" of creating intimacy or oneness in our marriages. Intimacy requires certain skills, which in tum call for a wholeness many of us do not possess. We need to counteract the loss of self-esteem and the competitiveness introduced into our sexual dynamics by postmodern culture, with a healthy self-understanding and a conceptual framework for intimacy in marriage.

In Chapter 2 we look at attitude and how it affects our success at the complex task of having successful intimacy with another human being. We will discover how attitudes are formed and how they can therefore be changed. I believe that if we are to alter our behaviour, it is essential that we first deal with our motivational centre: the "want to" must precede the "how to". This chapter also seeks to give a basic understanding of how the mind, and particularly the unconscious mind, operates and affects our day-to-day living.

Chapter 3 examines the way in which unresolved conflict from the past and negative conditioning from all the sources that have influenced us, affect our ability to operate in the present. Neglect and disillusionment have left us with a certain amount of hesitancy in entrusting ourselves emotionally to another person. We may need to acknowledge the very real emotional pain that such hurt and disillusionment has caused. This may in tum lead us to find a means of healing for our damaged emotions. Having dealt with past hurts, we will look at how to deal with current conflict. Most marriages do not disintegrate in one fiery blast or crisis, but are destroyed by the many small, unresolved conflicts that accumulate and erode our confidence in one another. We will look at practical steps for creating a conflict resolution model that will be effective for every kind of conflict, from how to squeeze the toothpaste to where to spend Christmas!

Chapter 4 is called "Of Heads and Hearts and Thinking Caps" and deals with models or concepts of marriage. Our view of marriage and our individual roles in marriage will determine the goals and ways of relating and behaving to which we will commit ourselves or accept as normative. In the hilarious movie "My Big Fat Greek Wedding", the Greek husband says: "I am the head of my home!" And his wife replied "Yes, but I'm the neck that turns the head!" Cultural models like this, supported by particular interpretations of biblical texts has caused many couples considerable pain. It has resulted in a view of marriage that breeds conflict and makes intimacy virtually impossible. This chapter seeks to remedy the situation by providing another interpretation of the data available to us. We will look quite intensively at those verses in the Bible as a major source of information.

Chapter 5 deals with goals and planning. It may seem strange to think in terms of planning for intimacy, but that is exactly what we need to do. The first stage of intimacy is friendship, and friends are people who have common goals and interests. We therefore need to develop skills in the area of setting mutual goals and planning our life of intimacy together. The complaint of many men and women is that the excitement and romance has disappeared from their marriages. As a result they seek these elsewhere. Some so-called "experts" even recommend an extra-marital affair as a means of revitalizing one's marriage! This is, in my view, oxymoronic advice! It is fallacious and extremely destructive to the dignity of marriage partners and the very fibre of the marriage. The alternative, however, is not to settle for a boring existence, but to plan your way to an ever-growing, exciting and fulfilling life of intimacy with your spouse!

In **Chapter 6,** "A Pedestal for *Eros*", we will examine how to restore and maintain romance by creating an environment in which erotic love can prosper and grow. I believe that the honeymoon phase of any marriage can be rekindled over and over again, and that the way to long-term success in marriage is to have many honeymoons with the same person. The way you treat your partner after marriage will determine the quality of your relationship. It follows that creativity in climate creation is therefore as important after the wedding as it is during courtship.

This leads us to **Chapter 7,** which looks at skills for creating intimacy. These include communication skills with the focus on the how and why of self-disclosure, particularly in the area of feelings. To consider one another means firstly that we understand each other. And understanding is not something that comes easily. It requires deliberate, conscientious engagement in the process of giving yourself to your partner and receiving her with gentleness.

In **Chapter 8** we deal with sexual skills. One of the common complaints of women, in particular, is that sex is engaged in without regard for the emotional environment in which it takes place. This raises the tricky subject of how men and women are wired sexually. I believe that sex is to be a consummation of intimacy, rather than a substitute for it. We need to be aware of the sexual games we so easily engage in, so that sex will be a means of upholding our partner's dignity and worth rather than an excuse for trampling it. Sex is one of the most beautiful forms of communication between two people. We can all improve our communication techniques. This chapter looks at how we can do this in the sexual area, and how we can be creative in our sexual practice within mamage.

We are going to cover a lot of ground in this short volume. Journey with me through the adventure of building a marriage characterized by intimacy, creativity and fun!

I want to thank the people who have made this book possible. My gratitude is due:

To God, the source of all truth, strength and life, who wants us to reign in life through the resources he has provided in Christ, and through His Word;

To my late parents, Jimmy and Anne, who lived a model of marriage that I have always tried to emulate.

To my wife, Lorraine, who as we approach our 50th anniversary, continues to amaze, fascinate and entrance me.

To my children, Justin, Melissa, Carmen and Candy, who have made us so proud, lived out their potential and demonstrated that the best thing any husband can do to ensure his children's future is to love their mother. I am so grateful for your love, belief, support and generosity, my precious family!

To Candy, a special mention and vote of thanks for your stirling work in getting this latest edition print-ready!

COSTA MITCHELL
November 2022

Chapter One

WHAT You SEE Is WHAT You GET

"What you see is what you get" is a popular American expression that means, if it is said of someone, that they are being completely honest. There is no cover-up, pretence or hidden agenda, and I can accept the person I am dealing with at face value. In this chapter I want to extend the phrase to include the idea that you *have to* see me in order to get me. In other words, *only what I show you of myself is truly yours.*

INTIMACY

This book is about intimacy. What is intimacy? Webster's defines it as "the state of being intimate". Intimate, from the Latin *intimus* for "innermost", means "belonging to, or sharing one's secret nature". A secret is something private, knowledge that I keep to myself and disclose only when and to whom I choose. Most of what I really am is secret. My values, beliefs, memories, dreams and feelings are unique to me and I only share them with those to whom I choose to disclose them. I don't remember where I first saw this excellent little play on words, but I use it all the time in my marriage courses. It goes "INTIMACY = INTO ME SEE"!

God intended intimacy to characterize marriage. The verb "to know" is used in the Bible to describe the sexual consummation of this relationship. For example, in Genesis 4: l we read that "Adam knew Eve his wife, and she conceived ... ". But intimacy is not just sexual consummation:

A minister colleague of mine was conducting a wedding, using the old form of service which asks the question: "If anyone can show any reason why these two may not be lawfully joined together, let him now speak, or forever hold his peace." My friend misspoke in the most hilarious spoonerism I've ever heard, and said "If anyone can show any reason why these two may not be joyfully loined together…!!!" It took a while for order and propriety to be restored!

So, again – intimacy is not just about the joining of loins, or sexual intercourse! It encompasses a *totality of knowing* that includes understanding how my partner thinks, and hearing her dreams and goals, values and feelings, what makes her happy or sad, loved and appreciated. Most importantly, intimacy is manifested when I walk in agreement with my partner, sharing her ambitions and fostering in her the sense that she is cherished and held in high regard, that I will support and encourage her in reaching those goals and dreams she cherishes. This level of emotional and psychological oneness is the basis of the true intimacy God designed for marriage. When sex is divorced from this understanding between husband and wife, it is reduced to an animal urge or lust that is demeaning to both partners. And, as it happens, the disillusionment it brings has been cited as among the top 3 most often quoted reasons for divorce.

Sexual intercourse that does not take place in the context of real emotional closeness with your partner leaves a sadness and sense of isolation. The experience of thousands of people bears this out. The modem trend of casual sexual liaison or living together without any sense of permanence is counter-intuitive for the human soul as God created it. As one woman put it: "I need to know that I belong to someone. Living together leaves me feeling insecure, as though he wants me at his convenience, but could stop wanting me at any moment, and then I would have to move out. I need him to make a commitment to me".

There are three steps to the process of becoming one, namely **Commitment, Communication** and **Consummation.**

Commitment is the first step toward oneness because it gives emotional safety to the individuals involved. This old-fashioned word expresses "an agreement or pledge to do something in the future"[1]; "dedicating yourself to something, like a person or a cause"[2]; or "strong belief in something; a promise to do something; enthusiasm; duty/responsibility".[3] It applies an individual's sense of honour and strength of character to whatever they are committed to do, so that you are saying, by the commitments you make, that "my word is attached to my name – if I break my word, you can consign my name to the garbage. I would rather die than break my promise".

This brings to mind the Biblical concept of a **Covenant** – an old concept of which we would do well to remind ourselves. The model is most often used in relation to God's relationship with His people, but in using it, God borrows from the culture of the time. It was applied to the relationship between kings and their subjects, between business partners, between families, friends, bands of soldiers, and of course, between husbands and wives. As I describe the concept, its symbols and their meanings, please think about their application to your marriage relationship.

When two parties entered into a covenant, they would stand opposite one another and do the following things:

- They would remove and exchange their belts, which held their swords and their money bags. They would accompany this exchange with words of pledge, expressing their commitment to protect and provide for the other: When two people marry,

[1] Merriam-Webster Dictionary
[2] The Oxford online Dictionary
[3] McMillan online Dictionary

they are saying to each other "Your enemies are my enemies, your battles are my battles. I will defend you against all threats, and my strength and wealth will be for your provision."

- They would remove and exchange their outer coats, which, much like Scottish tartan clothing, carried the colours of their respective tribes, clans and families. In this exchange they would be saying: "I take your identity and honour, and give you mine". This would also usually involve the taking of one another's names in some form, either as a middle name or incorporating one name into the other. An example of the latter is how "Abram" becomes "Abr(yah)am" after God enters a covenant with him. This is still the practice in most marriages, although usually, only the wife takes the husband's name (where that should probably be more like it used to be, when couples would take one another's names).

- The two parties would then cut the name of the other into the palm of their right hands, and clasp hands while the blood of both mingled in their clasped palms. The result was a permanent scar in the form of the name of any covenant partner being seen if a person held up their right hand, which they would do when making an oath or pledge, or before engaging in battle. What the person did publicly after entering a covenant, they did "in the name" of those whose name they thus carried. When it comes to marriage, these days rings are worn to signify this idea.

- Finally, (if you will excuse the graphic details!) they would kill an animal and cut it in two pieces. The pieces would be laid on the ground a few metres apart, and the parties would link arms and walk in a figure of eight between the pieces, reciting the terms of their covenant agreement, and adding "If I should ever break my word to you, may my life be forfeit as that of this animal." In vivid symbolism, they proclaimed that they were entering into a death and were journeying into a new life. They were dying to self-interest and passing through that death to a new relationship of union with the other party to the covenant.[4] The vows couples make to one another in the wedding ceremony are the closest equivalent to this practice. They express the content of the intention of each to live for the benefit of their union, and of one another. A beautiful example of this kind of expression is one that was expressed between a woman (Ruth) and her mother-in-law (Naomi). Both women had been widowed by a plague, and Naomi was going to go back to her parental homeland. She tells her two daughters-in-law to stay behind and seek new husbands, but Ruth speaks the most beautiful words of covenant commitment in the whole of the Bible, saying: "Don't ask me to leave you and turn back. Wherever you go, I will go; wherever you live, I will live. Your people will be my people, and your God will be my God. Wherever you die, I will die, and there I will be buried. May the LORD punish me severely if I allow anything but death to separate us!"[5]

❖ The covenant would be sealed by a meal in which bread and wine were shared. The marriage "feast" or reception is the continued symbolic fulfilment of this practice.

I inserted a quote above from a book called *"The Power of the Blood Covenant"* by Malcolm Smith, which has been a great source of information on this subject of covenants and their significance. He defines a covenant as follows:

> A covenant is a binding, unbreakable obligation between two parties, based on unconditional love sealed by blood and sacred oath, that creates a relationship in which each party is bound by specific undertakings on each other's behalf. The parties to the covenant place themselves under

---

[4] Smith, Malcolm. The Power of the Blood Covenant (pp. 18-19). Harrison House Publishers. Kindle Edition.

[5] Ruth 1:16-17 New Living Translation

> the penalty of divine retribution should they later attempt to avoid those undertakings. It is a relationship that can only be broken by death.[6]

Smith further explains the important distinction between the idea of covenant and its closest modern equivalent of a *contract*, which many take to be the same thing as a covenant. Smith says "Contracts are negotiable by both of the parties and can be changed or even cancelled. In a contract, promises are made that are as good as the character of the contracting parties whose signatures seal the document; therefore, they are easily broken. A covenant is totally different. A covenant is far above the exchange of properties and things. It is the giving of one's whole person and life to another and the wholehearted receiving of that other person and his or her life."[7]

Why all of this is important, in the context of marriage, is that this kind of commitment is what gives marriage its power. My maternal grandmother used to use a common Afrikaans expression when talking about marriage: *"Trou is nie perde koop nie!"* which translates into "Marriage is not like buying a horse!" It is not a bargain or deal you make, or a 50/50 compromise arrangement. It is not something you agree to until a better offer comes around. Covenant partners are not disposable on a whim. Rather, covenant requires both parties to be "all in". I usually tell the couples I marry, at some point in the marriage ceremony, "Today, you are signing your death warrant!" I want them to understand that, in choosing marriage, they are choosing to live a selfless life, committed to live for the wellbeing of the other, at the cost of their own wellbeing if necessary.[8]

In a later chapter we will look at the meaning of the Greek word for "love" that is used most often in the New Testament, but let me say

---

[6] Smith, Malcolm. The Power of the Blood Covenant (p. 13).

[7] Smith, Malcolm. The Power of the Blood Covenant (p. 17). Harrison House Publishers. Kindle Edition.

[8] Psalm 15:4, for example, speaks about a virtuous person, among other things, as one "who keeps his word even when it hurts and does not change".

here that the word beautifully represents what covenant does, in that it describes love that acts for the wellbeing of the beloved one, to the point of dying for them. It is well understood as unconditional commitment to an imperfect person. The more imperfect the person loved, the more of this love is drawn out of the lover. It is love that will never quit. It exists as long as the lover does. The commitment made is based on the character, or honour, of the one making it. Until you have "got over yourself", and moved past what you're entitled to, it is impossible to sustain. However, the opposite is also true. The greatest wellbeing you will ever know is what you experience when you are seeking the wellbeing of the other.

On the receiver's side of this kind of commitment is a safety for which the soul has been searching. Think of a trapeze artist, expressing her artistry between trapezes 30 metres above ground, but with a safety net below her. Being able to feel that "no failure is fatal" empowers her to fully express her talent without fear, with creativity and freedom. So it is when a person feels unconditionally loved. Free to give, free to enjoy, free to express their love for the one who loves them. This is the love that heals and releases the full potential of each person loved in this way.

The second step to the union between two people in marriage is **Communication**, the process of sharing thoughts, beliefs, hopes, dreams, fears, joys and other feelings that make each of us unique. When communication forms part of marital union, it expresses the desire for more than physical closeness. I will discuss this in more detail in a future chapter, but suffice it here to say that making common to someone else what is "inside me" is essential to that person being able to "into-me-see"!

Dennis Rainey, in his book *Lonely Husbands, Lonely Wives*,[9] discusses the differences in sexual orientation and experience between men and women. Some would regard his views as sexist -

[9] Dennis Rainey, *Lonely Husbands, Lonely Wives: Rekindling Intimacy in Every Marriage* (Milton Keynes: Word (UK), 1990), p. 255.

he himself warns against overgeneralization - but I believe we would be foolish to disregard well-researched information about sexual or gender differences in the cause of sexual equality. Equality does not mean uniformity. Rainey highlights the fact that women are more sensitive than men to emotional environment and true intimacy through understanding, attitudes, words, touch and the actions leading up to sexual intercourse. I believe that men need to learn from their partners and become more sensitive in these areas, not for their wives' sake but for their own. Marriage makes for more than "the two becoming one" – it also makes for each one becoming whole, as we learn from the strengths of the other, and grow through our individual limitations and blind spots. The apostle Peter calls men to their obligations in marriage with these words: "In the same way, you husbands must give *honour* to your wives. Treat your wife with *understanding* (or '*consideration*') as you live together." To be considerate requires spending time, listening with respect, hearing with a desire to truly understand.

Socrates shared one of the secrets of happiness or fulfilment in his famous dictum: Know thyself. What he did not say was that knowing myself and being known by someone else are inextricably bound up. I can only truly know myself and therefore come to wholeness or fulfilment to the extent that I engage in a mutually self-disclosing relationship with another human being.

The Johari Window (Diagram 2) shows the four dimensions of selfhood found in every person. My "Public Self' is the part of me that is known to me and to others. My "Blind Self' is known to others but not to me. My "Private Self' is known to me but unknown to others, and my "Unknown Self' is hidden from both me and others.

In intimate self-disclosure with another person, I reveal things about myself that no one knows but me. My Public Self is extended to replace a part of my Private Self. A part of my Private Self is therefore being revealed. When this happens, I am inviting feedback from the other person. Her response tells me things about myself that I did not know, and my Blind Self is diminished as my Public Self grows.

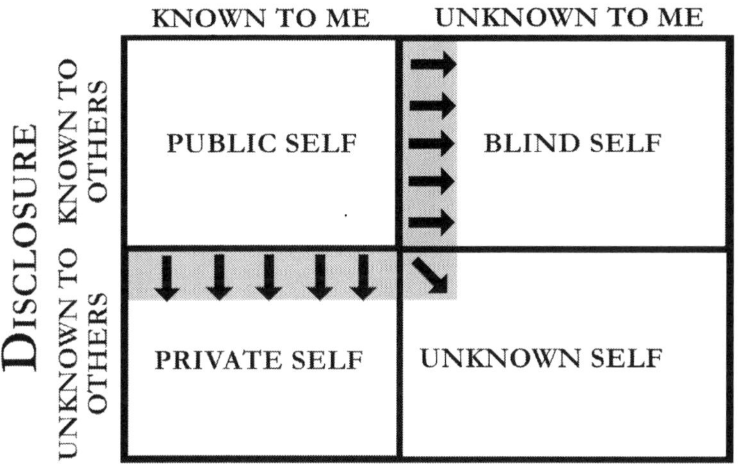

(The shaded area grows as the arrows of disclosure and feedback move outward in the diagram.) Notice too that as my Public Self grows, it affects my Unknown Self. Aspects of myself that could never have been discovered otherwise, potentials that would never have been realized, are liberated and fulfilled as I grow to wholeness through self-disclosure. There is no other way in which we can become whole. Risky as it may be, being real with my partner is the way God has designed for me to achieve my full potential. It is in a meaningful, committed, selfdisclosing relationship with a member of the opposite sex that I achieve wholeness.

It is important to remember that meaningful selfdisclosure is not to be engaged in carelessly or expected from others too quickly. There is something undignified about people who impose their innermost secrets on others before they have earned the right or been invited to do so. However, the opposite danger is the more common one. The Greek philosopher Aristotle can be credited with (or blamed for!) most of the distinctive character and attitudes, culture and ways of functioning (ethos) of the Western world. Without making this too complicated, it will help us to understand ourselves and our world if we know where our basic world-view originated.

Aristotle created categories of reason or thought. He divided animal life into genus and species, and human life and interest into ten clearly distinct categories. He emphasised reason or rational thought as the highest ability of man and said it was to be separated from religion.[10] His categories became compartments of thought and life that were further developed by the scholasticism that dominated medieval western Europe. They eventually became entrenched in the "faculties" or departments of learning at universities. For centuries Western society has therefore been conditioned to see rationalism as the highest value and to attempt to divide reason from faith in God and the emotions. The rational or ideal man is thought to be undermined by emotion or affection.

It is fairly easy to see the impact of this kind of thinking on our lives today. It has had a major influence on religion, but more important to the subject of marriage and intimacy is the effect it has had on our emotional orientation as WASPs - White Anglo-Saxon Protestants. Aristotle's categories developed into the generalizations of Victorian England that have left us a legacy that teaches that displays of emotion (or even admitting that we have them!) are not socially acceptable. The virtue of the stiff upper lip has been extolled to an extreme that robs us of our humanity in the very important area of our emotions. This has had a particularly detrimental effect on men. "Cowboys don't cry" epitomizes the attitude of many Western males towards emotion and the expression of feelings. To be a real man means that you do not show your emotions, especially not tenderness, vulnerability, insecurity, sadness or fear. This distorted view of the importance of emotions, and therefore of self-disclosure, is exacerbated by two factors: The first - low self-esteem, is common to all relationships; the second - the war between the sexes, affects marriage in particular.

[10] Encyclopaedia Britannica Macropaedia, Volume 1, p. 1167.

THE IMPORTANCE OF HEALTHY SELF ESTEEM

One of the most powerful driving forces of human motivation is an attitude we call the "Self Concept", which incorporates two things: Self Image (The person we think we are – a picture of ourselves we see in an internal "mirror") and Self Esteem (the value or price tag we attach to that person we think we are). Most people do not feel good about themselves. For many the truthful answer to the question: "How much would you pay for yourself?" is: "Not very much". However, rather than admit this, we visualize an ideal self and then spend time, energy and money trying to make ourselves into that image. We design and make masks and hide behind them as we interact with others. If we succeed in doing this, we will, in all likelihood, gain friends and even a marriage partner who likes, respects and loves the image we have created. The rest of life becomes a long struggle to prop up the image and prevent anyone from seeing the real me.

Our emotions form part of who we really are. We do not like them because they are an admission of weakness and represent an area we do not fully control. We therefore do not want to disclose them to anyone else. John Powell has written a marvellous little volume called "Why Am I Afraid to Tell You Who I Am?". His answer to this question is simply that I do not like who I am. To tell you who I am would incur the risk of your rejection because you might not like me either.[11]

In the Biblical story of Adam and Eve there is a great parallel to what Powell describes. They had been made in God's image, and described as "perfect!" Then they declare themselves independent of the Creator, and decide to design their own purpose. That evening, God comes to enjoy intimacy with his creatures "in the cool of the day", as is his habit. But the couple are not waiting eagerly for their daily exchange. One of the most pathetic verses in the Bible has

[11] John S. J. Powell, Why Am I Afraid to Tell You Who I Am? (Allen: Tabor Publishing, 1969).

God calling for them: "Where are you?" God finds them hiding in the shrubbery and asks why they are hiding. Their reply expresses so much of the common human state: " ... I was afraid because I was naked; and I hid myself". The conversation continues, with God asking "Who told you that you were naked?" And Adam's reply is a classic, as he says: "The *woman You gave me* made me do it!"

In psychological language, what is displayed is the creation of a series of defence mechanisms, like avoidance, masking or imaging, projection and blame-shifting. We still employ these devices in the conduct of the social dance of relationship, including marriage. Through them we attempt to hide our low self-esteem, or try to make ourselves acceptable by appearing normal, creating a "me" that blends in with the shrubbery. The fashion industry is built on this principle, predicated on the desire to be "fashionable". While the tendency to try and find our identity in a peer group is a normal part of growing up, many people never grow past this stage.

Many a marriage has fallen victim, not to major destructive events like extramarital affairs, but to the slow poison of either party never really "getting" their spouse, but a disguised alter-ego, to whom they must relate, so that a marriage that was meant to create "into-me-see" has merely caused frustration and isolation. They are crying out to their partners, sometimes in outlandish ways: "Where are you?"

Research has shown that the greatest fear of 80% of people is to be asked to speak in front of more than five people. It is a greater fear for most than the fear of dying – meaning that most people would rather be the corpse at a funeral than the person giving the eulogy! We fear exposure because we do not like what we see in the mirror. If this is true of most of us physically speaking, how much more is it true of our emotional state? We are afraid of the feelings that lurk beneath the surface and of emotion itself. We are afraid of the loss of control that emotional behaviour represents and of the weakness we believe it demonstrates. So we cover ourselves with our inadequate little aprons of leaves, oblivious of the fact that many of the leaves have dropped off, and that, as the frustration of loneliness intensifies, we will become more and more exposed until we stand quite naked, and afraid, before people who will reject what they see.

The anonymous poem "The Wall' describes graphically the process and the danger of emotional neglect in marriage:

Their wedding picture mocked them from the table,
These two whose lives no longer touched each other.
They loved with such a heavy barricade between them
That neither battering ram of words nor artilleries of touch could break it down.
Somewhere between the oldest child's first tooth and the youngest daughter's graduation, They lost each other.

Throughout the years each slowly unravelled that tangled ball of string called self
and as they tugged at stubborn knots, each hid his searching from the other.
Sometimes she cried at night, and begged the whispering darkness to tell her who she was
while he lay beside her, snoring like a hibernating bear, unaware of her winter.
Once, after they had made love, he wanted to tell her how afraid he was of dying.

But fearing to show his naked soul, he spoke instead about the beauty of her breasts.
She took a course in modern art, trying to find herself in colours splashed upon a canvas
And complaining to other women about men who were insensitive.
He climbed into a tomb called "The Office", wrapped his mind in a shroud of paper figures and buried himself in customers.

Slowly, the wall between them rose, cemented by the mortar of indifference.
One day, reaching out to touch each other,
They found a barrier they could not penetrate
And, recoiling from the coldness of the stone, each retreated from the stranger on the other side.

For when love dies, it is not in a moment of angry battle,
Nor when fiery bodies lose their heat;
It lies, panting, exhausted, expiring
At the bottom of a wall it could not scale.

THE WAR BETWEEN THE SEXES

The second factor that hinders our self-disclosure in marriage is the war between the sexes. The sexual revolution, and especially the feminist movement, has resulted in fierce competitiveness characterizing the relationships between men and women.

Women felt, and still feel, the need to be acknowledged and equally remunerated for doing jobs previously "reserved" for men. As one woman said, in order to compete in a man's world and get the same recognition, a woman needs to be twice as good as a man. "But then," she added, "that's only half as difficult as it sounds!"

There is obviously much that is good and healthy in the feminist movement. The recognition of women's rights in terms of equality before the law, in the work place, civil society and in marriage has been long overdue. However, we need to be aware of the tendency in this movement, as in all liberation movements, towards overreaction. This is manifested in the blurring of gender roles and in the militancy and "reverse sexism" of its current forms.

In marriage this influence is seen in the heavy emphasis that is placed on the individual and her or his needs, goals, career and rights, so that the couple's goals and needs and the development of what has been called a "couple personality" are neglected. When the war between the sexes is carried into the marriage space, intimacy becomes impossible. If l see my partner as a competitor, I will not be able to disclose my feelings and vulnerable areas to him. No one wants her rival to know her weaknesses!

The biblical purpose of marriage is oneness. " This explains why a man leaves his father and mother and is joined to his wife, and the two are united into one." (Genesis 2:24 NLT). The Hebrew word for "one" used in this verse refers to a composite unity - a unity that consists of more than one person, but that produces a blending of persons into a mysterious and wonderful unity. It literally means that the two shall become one person. The antidote to growing isolation and an exclusive focus on selfhood is therefore the understanding that it is both God's plan for me, and eminently possible, to achieve intimacy in marriage through self-giving. This will not threaten my personhood. In fact if I handle it in the context of a secure, positive Self-Concept, it will provide the means for my completion.

The Genesis statement I referenced above is repeated in Jesus' teaching about marriage in Matthew 19:5 and in Paul's elaboration on the subject in Ephesians 5:31, and is implied in the prophetic book of Malachi 2:15[12] as well! I get the impression that God really wants us to get the message! He reiterates it to emphasise its importance – and time has not altered his original plan for marriage. Marriage is not a convenience created purely for my pleasure, although pleasure and happiness lie at the end of fulfilled purpose. That purpose is for me to experience deep, growing, multi-faceted oneness with my partner. Oneness does not happen in a moment, nor is it purely sexual union, but rather a process leading to the totality of knowing I mentioned earlier.

The gift of sexuality is part of the image of God in us. In the Genesis account of creation we read that God created us" ... in his own image; in the image of God he created him; male and female he created them" (Genesis 1 :27). The separation of humanity on the basis of gender followed the creation of a single human being. That person contained the image of God, which means that the nature or disposition of God was internalised in him. What that nature was and is, is the subject of some debate in Christian theology, but for the purposes of this book it is important to understand that the essential nature of God is love. And love cannot exist in a vacuum. It seeks expression, as it did in God's acts of creation and His repeated attempts to draw people into intimacy with Himself, culminating in the passion and drama of the cross.

[12] Didn't the LORD make you one with your wife? In body and spirit you are His. …So guard your heart; remain loyal to the wife of your youth. (NLT)

Our built-in desire for love and oneness, or God's image in us, is the key to the mysterious motivation towards intimacy that fascinates and plagues most of us. The phrase "the image of God" forms an emphatic parallel to the phrase "male and female" (verse 27). God divided the image along gender lines, leaving each partner with the full potential to express God, yet with the yearning for the completion of his humanity through the reuniting of the divided race. I carry the image of God within me as an individual, but some of it is hidden in the "otherness" of my partner. There are aspects of the image of God in me that can only be discovered in the adventure of becoming one with my marriage partner. This means that true oneness is not a loss of personhood or uniqueness. In fact, I only discover my true uniqueness in mutual self-giving with my partner.

My maleness does not lie in performing certain roles, nor is it lost by performing others that have been thought of as "women's work". The same applies to femaleness. Sexuality, in emotional and psychological terms, is a style or mode of being. When I express that style, I am manifesting my uniqueness and giving something of that style to my wife. Carl Jung spoke of the masculine style in terms of directedness or goal-orientation, or what he called a "doing" mode. When I live out my maleness in my home in this way, I share it with my wife and she discovers a wholeness she did not experience on her own.

My wife, on the other hand, expresses a uniquely feminine style in whatever she does. In this way she in tum gives something to me that I would not even have seen without her. Jung spoke of the feminine in terms of a "being" mode, a sense of wholeness or a diffuse, allencompassing connection with life.[13] When my wife lives out her unique femininity she is a reminder, a lesson to my maleness, that to be gentle is as vital to my humanity as it is to be successful. When these styles of being are expressed in the security of a marriage relationship, there need be no competitiveness or fear

[13] Carl Jung "Structural Forms of the Feminine Psyche", quoted by Dr Toni Grant, Being a Woman (New York: Random House, 1988), pp. 22 -23.

that my vulnerability will be exploited. It is rather a celebration of my own and my partner's uniqueness, and a discovery by each of the wholeness of being human.

In my experience, the main reason why men do not disclose their feelings is the fear that their wives will lose respect for them. The reality is, however, quite the opposite. Men who disclose their feelings to their wives not only find that their wives respect them more for doing so, but that such self-disclosure proves to be a means to the most fulfilling and beautiful intimacy or oneness they could desire. The following extract from a letter from a wife who experienced this new respect for and intimacy with her husband illustrates the point. (I have obviously changed their names):

> The more John gets in touch with his own feelings, the more he is able to share with me, and the more I am able to enter into his world and become one with him. As we have learned to make ourselves vulnerable to each other and keep our defences down, it has brought about warm, loving feelings and helped to generate sexual chemistry and physical oneness between us.

If it is true that what you see is what you get, and that you only see what I allow you to see, the adventure and challenge of marriage is to enable your partner see the real you. In the process you become whole, your partner receives a whole, real person rather than a plastic replica, and together you experience in your marriage an intimacy that gives full expression to the phrase, "they shall become one flesh".

Chapter Two

IT'S MOSTLY IN THE "WANT TO"

Marriage is the coming together of two people in a commitment to live together, love each other, endure, enjoy and become one. Each of these two people is a complex being with unique thoughts, emotions, likes and dislikes, beliefs, memories and values, lifestyle and patterns of behaviour. To understand how marriage works we therefore need to know how the individual operates. How does the mind function? Where do emotions come from? How can they be controlled? What makes me and my partner tick? What are attitudes?

Success at any venture requires three basic ingredients: knowledge, skill and the right attitude. What does each of these factors contribute to my success? The surprising answer is that knowledge forms 10%, skill 15% and attitude an amazing 75% of the total recipe for success. Whether we are dealing with life in general, managing a business, closing a sale or trying to succeed at marriage, we need to bear these statistics in mind. A person with all the knowledge and skills necessary to succeed at a task will be only 25% successful if he has a negative attitude, while someone who has the right attitude but only minimal skill and knowledge can be 75% successful. We will consider some important attitudes in this chapter: self-concept, self-esteem, commitment, positiveness and tolerance.

ATTITUDES

Attitudes are conscious and subconscious habits of thought. They affect our ability to make a commitment and to focus on any task or venture and follow it through to successful completion. To understand this better, think of knowledge as the **What**, skill as the **How To** and attitude as the **Want To** of any activity. While no one gets married without consciously *wanting* the relationship to succeed, we may subconsciously carry a "wide open back door" attitude that says "if it doesn't make me feel good, I'll get out". This is an example of a "want to" with a BUT – terms and conditions apply!

Other attitudes are more subtle but no less important to success. They may even be more influential because we are unaware of them. We can never completely hide our attitudes. They are revealed by unguarded words, actions and body language. They create responses in people and contribute to the overall impression we make on others.

Psychologists use the phrase: "You do not act like the person you are, but like the person you think you are". King Solomon predates this wisdom by a few thousand years when he writes: "For as he thinks in his heart, so is he" (Proverbs 23: 7). The way I think about myself reveals my attitude to or habit of thought about myself. This, as I pointed out in the previous chapter, is my *Self Concept*. It is like an internal mirror reflecting the me I perceive myself to be. The value, or price tag, that I attach to this reflection is what we call *Self Esteem*. The level of my self-esteem can in turn determine many other attitudes, such as whether I am an introvert or an extrovert, positive or negative, an optimist or a pessimist. These are all habits of thought. Think about your habits. We all have them - some good, like exercising, good manners and cleanliness, and some bad, like smoking and overeating. However, unless we are born to a mother with a mainline heroin addiction, we are not born with any habits! They are acquired by performing certain actions a number of times in succession until they become automatic responses to certain stimuli. Attitudes or habits of thought operate in precisely the same way. We are not born with them but allow them to form through a process of repetitive thinking or behaviour.

FORMING ATTITUDES

The human mind is like a computer. And, as anyone with any knowledge of computers will tell you, a computer is like a blank page. It contains nothing until someone feeds data into it. That is why computer people use the expression *"Garbage In, Garbage Out"*. A computer has input and output terminals (keyboard, printer and screen) and a data base (the computer itself). Whatever input I key into the data base will be displayed as output on the screen or in print. If l had a new computer and programmed it to the effect that 2 + 2 = 7, it would always compute the sum in that way. Every time you asked it to add 2 + 2, or multiples thereof, it would give the answer 7. A newborn baby has a mind like a computer with very little programming- "very little" would include unconscious awareness and experiences from the months before birth and the birth process itself. When this little life is entrusted into the care of a family, the writing of the programme begins.

Some babies are "programmed" more easily than others, for reasons still unexplained. At nine months my son found electrical sockets fascinating, especially because the holes were exactly finger size. He would toddle across the room, hand outstretched, and stick his finger into the hole. If we caught him at it, we would say, "No, Justin!" and emphasise our displeasure with a tap of two fingers on the offending hand.

You could literally see his thought process, as he stopped and frowned: "Oh, wrong finger!" And he would try another... "No, Justin!" (smack)... "Oh, wrong hand!" The left hand index finger would go for the hole. "No, Justin!" (smack). "Oh, wrong ***plug!***" And he would scoot across to the plug on the other side of the room to repeat the process... It took Justin's computer a while to register that it was not a good idea to put a finger from either hand into any plug anywhere in any room, in any house!

A computer stores whatever data we feed into it and will never lose that information. The same applies to our minds. We store every memory of every experience or every piece of information we have perceived and paid attention to in our lifetime in our human data base, the *Unconscious* or, as it is more popularly called, our *Subconscious* mind.

CONSCIOUS AND SUBCONSCIOUS MIND

The diagram below illustrates the relationship between the conscious and the subconscious mind, and the roles each plays in the motivation process. The conscious mind is the input terminal, with the functions of **Perception** (becoming aware through the senses), **Cognition** (understanding or interpreting), **Evaluation** (attaching value to or judging) and **Volition** or decision-making.

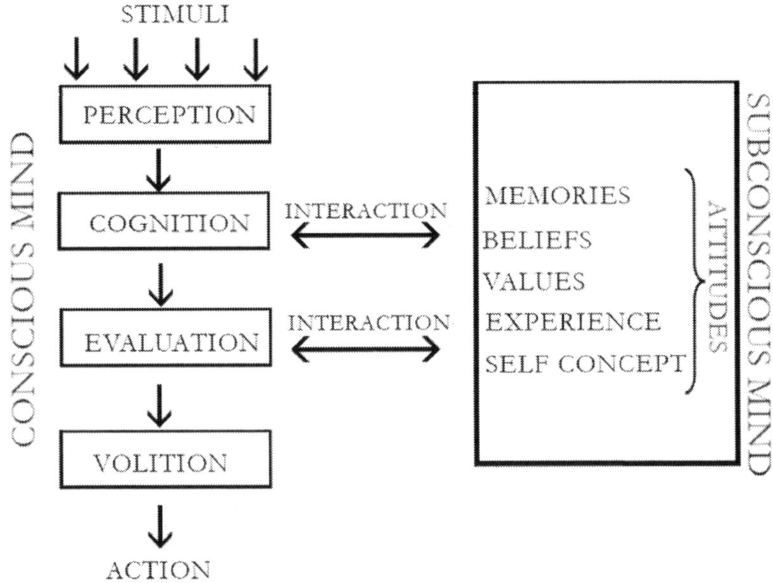

Any stimulus begins the process and a fairly orderly procedure is followed with some interaction at every stage between the conscious mind and the subconscious mind. This is especially true of the cognition and evaluation stages. (See the arrows in the diagram.)

The subconscious mind is the data base. It has on file every memory, belief, value and experience as well as our self-concept. These together form our *"want to"*, and play a crucial part in the decision-making process. Interactions between conscious and subconscious take place in a split second. The human output device is our behaviour. We reveal our attitudes by what we do. Of course, we also have conscious data, information or thoughts that help us make reasoned decisions about what we want to commit ourselves to and see in our lives and marriages. As we begin to realize what our "want to" is going to cost, we seek information in the data base to help us decide whether this is worth doing or not.

It is important to note that only 10% of my decisions are derived from the conscious mind-the remaining 90% are contributed by the subconscious! What happens when there is a serious difference of opinion? In decision-making, as in boxing, Rugby, American Football or any other contest where size or weight is important, the big guy usually wins! This explains why we often feel guilty about implementing decisions we are responsible for. We are like a city divided against itself. For most of us there is a constant argument between our conscious and subconscious minds, or the thoughts (conscious) and intentions (subconscious) of our hearts.

We were not born with any information in our subconscious minds. It was gathered through childhood experiences, particularly in the first six years of life. The answer to the question: "Why are some people more positive (friendly, tolerant) than others?" is, for the most part, simply that they were taught or programmed to be so. While we all have some genetically derived characteristics, most researchers agree that by far the greater determinant in attitude development and responses to life is experience. This comprises not only precepts we are taught but especially the behaviour and responses modelled by emotionally significant persons in our lives. It is patently true, as the anonymous poet says, that "A Child Learns What He Lives":

If a child lives with criticism, he learns to condemn;
If he lives with hostility,
he learns to fight.
If a child lives with ridicule, he learns to be shy;
If he lives with shame,
he learns to feel guilty.
If a child lives with tolerance,
he learns to be patient;
If he lives with encouragement,
he learns to have confidence.
If a child lives with praise,
he learns to appreciate;
If he lives with fairness,
he learns justice.
If a child lives with security,
he learns to have faith;
If he lives with approval,
he learns to like himself.
And; If a child lives with acceptance and friendship,
he learns to find love in the world.

Our subject in this book is marriage, but let us reflect for a moment on these thoughts about parenthood. A large amount of the counselling or emotional healing ministry exercised in a wide range of churches, concentrates on repairing the damage done in childhood by the actions and attitudes of parents. We are entrusted with an awesome responsibility as stewards of the impressionable lives of our children. The wealth of information and help available today leaves us no excuse for failure. And it is probably never more true than in this vital area, that an ounce of prevention is better than a pound of cure - and a lot easier!

I have seen parents who are successful in their own right, but their achievements make them intolerant of one or more of their children, undermine their children's self-esteem and produce negative attitudes in them. Conversely, people born with physical and mental handicaps, such as learning disabilities, have become household names through the careful nurture of positive attitudes such as self-esteem, initiative and determination. Winston Churchill was told by a school teacher that he would never amount to much.[14] Albert Einstein had a learning disability[15] and Thomas Edison's mother was told "your boy is addled (mentally deficient)".[16] Through a combination of acceptance and affirmation from parents and others they admired, and positive "self-talk", they generated the right attitudes and succeeded at their chosen life tasks.

SELF CONCEPT

One of the most important attitudes we can cultivate is a positive self-concept. Most people I meet have negative self-esteem. Positive self-esteem is developed through being able to say two things, repeatedly and with integrity: "I am loved" and "I am competent".

"I am loved" is a statement of intrinsic, unconditional value. The young child has to perceive this message in the home environment. Before six years of age they have no internal mirror by which to judge themselves. Their perception of self and the resultant value they attribute to that self is drawn from the way parents and other emotionally significant persons respond to them. Deposits are made in the bank of a child's self-esteem when others acknowledge their existence and pay them attention.

Such acknowledgements are called "strokes".[17] A hug, a smile, the touch of a hand or a word of praise or affirmation is a positive stroke; a blow, a hurtful word, a rebuke or physical abuse is a negative stroke. The volume of the one versus the other in a child's first six years will largely determine the currency she will expect to be paid in for the rest of her life.

---

[14] Encyclopaedia Britannica Macropaedia (1974), Volume 4, p.20595

[15] Encyclopaedia Britannica Macropaedia (1974), Volume 6, p.20511.

[16] U.S> Library of Congress Biography of Thomas Alva Edison

[17] T.A. Harris, *I'm 0.K., You're O.K.* (London: Jonathan Cape, 1973), p. 41.

As a child grows, the place from which they get their strokes changes. In the years between age 6 and 12, my Peers are the source of strokes. When I am included in gangs, teams and quality time spent, the sense of being loved and accepted is reinforced and grows. In the years between 12 and 18, the mirror of self-image is internalised, so that who I am in my own estimation becomes the important measure of self-concept.

When we enter the world of seeking and courting a life partner, most of us need and are drawn in the mate selection process to someone who reinforces our self-esteem. When my internal bank balance is low, I use others (and especially my spouse) as an auto-teller to draw from to replenish my emotional resources. The mature adult will have arrived, before marriage, at a sense of self that is independently whole and healthy. However, there is always going to be a sense in which our spouse is a source of reinforcing our self-esteem, holding up a mirror that says: "Here you are safe, accepted and loved."

SELF ESTEEM

We said that it is necessary to say "I am competent" to develop and maintain positive self-esteem. The day we are born, a wonderful journey of growth, adventure, risk-taking and discovery begins. We learn that we can climb out of our cot and survive! Then the house becomes our frontier. We cross it to explore the garden, and again we survive. Next comes the adventure of getting out of the garden. And so the frontier-crossing or goal achievement continues. Whether it is a little thing like tying your own laces or riding your bike for the first time without falling off, passing a grade at school, being chosen for a sports team, closing your first deal or making your first million, the feeling is the same. It is the feeling called success. It says: I did it! I can do it! I am competent! But this only applies to a goal that you set and achieve yourself. Winning a million on the lottery, or marrying into success and money will not do it for us. Being able to say "I am competent" is a function of personal goal achievement, and we need it on a daily basis. Our achievements from last year or last month or even yesterday will not do the trick today. Self-esteem cannot be stored up. It needs daily reinforcement.

Because our attitudes, values and self-concept are contained in the subconscious mind, it is possible for them to work against each other. This inner conflict can virtually tear us apart emotionally. I believe that some of these values are built in because we are made in God's image. No amount of social conditioning or denial can eradicate or silence them. They speak to us constantly, sometimes in judgment and sometimes in affirmation of our behaviour. Let us look at an example of this.

Joe has values that tell him that it is important to be honest, hard-working and disciplined. These values are developed in his subconscious mind through the influence of his family and his experiences over the first years of his life. But Joe also has habits of thought acquired later in life. He has learned that it is more pleasurable to avoid responsibility, honesty and discipline. His attitudes therefore result in choices of behaviour that are at odds with his value system. The "oughts" are overwhelmed by the reality of "if it feels good, do it". Does Joe get away with this? Emphatically not! The internal judge and jury are in session, and the basis of judgment is his value system. Joe feels guilty, his self-esteem is eroded and the person that he thinks he is, is diminished. He lives in a state we call "cognitive dissonance". His emotional energy will be diminished. He will have even less chance of behaving in a way that upholds his value system next time around.

This is the unfortunate and all too familiar downward spiral that entraps all of us to some extent. The biblical command to "love your neighbour as yourself' is more than a command. It is a statement of fact. We do love our neighbour as ourselves, but most of us love ourselves negatively or, at best, conditionally - we feel good about ourselves when we are doing well or looking good. And we love others in the same way. What is even more tragic is that we cannot accept love from others if we do not love ourselves. We sabotage their attempts to love us rather than have them contradict our self-concept.

ATTITUDES AND INTIMACY

Let us think about the impact of these attitudes on marriage, and how to change them. The focus of this book is not on marriage or on staying married, but rather on leading a fulfilled married life through the enjoyment of intimacy. Success at this goal is a function of the three basic ingredients we spoke about at the beginning of the chapter: knowledge, skill and the right attitude. While skill and knowledge play a part, our success at creating intimacy is determined by our attitude. Do we really want to have intimacy with our spouse? I am not talking about having sex or making love, but of cultivating a "vibe" and maintaining the chemistry of attraction, openness, communication and sharing that gives value to each partner and joy to their union.

Most of us know how to do that, at least well enough to have secured exclusive commitment from another person in the first place. We may need a little help to understand what real intimacy is. But most marriages become boring, unfulfilling prisons because the "want to" has faded. It is the lack of "want to" that turns a charming suitor into an uncaring, slobby chauvinist and a vivacious, stimulating beauty into an unkempt, cynical bore. The person who started out on the journey is still in there somewhere - she comes out when there is a school reunion dinner or some such "need to impress" event. When there is a strong enough "want to", the resident fairy godmother is not far away from Cinderella (or Cinderfella, as the case may be!) If you really want to, you can turn on the old charm for your wife of 20 years or for your ageing husband whose bifocals provide the only glint in his eye.

However, what actually happens in something like 50% of marriages today, is that somewhere between the first baby's second tooth and the husband's most exciting promotion at the age of 45, the spark is extinguished. The intimacy that drew the couple together is pushed aside by the fight for identity or gets bogged down in the nappy bucket. The husband's already brittle self-concept, in need of reinforcement at home because of the battering it took when his fifth sales call in a row drew a blank, comes home to a woman whose emotional bank balance is in overdraft. The unrewarding routine of a young mother's busy day leaves her feeling that she really does not amount to much. He comes to this autoteller for a payout and she either says, "We're sorry- funds are not available from this account" or, on particularly bad days, gobbles up his card and spits it out in little pieces. The display reads: "Why should I make you feel good when I feel so lousy?"

This situation can be, and often is, reversed. A tired, irritable husband comes home to a wife whose day has left her in need of loving affirmation. It is usually couched in innocent-sounding code.

"Please talk to me." (I need intimacy.)

"In a moment. I just want to catch up with the sports channel first." (This TV is more interesting than you.)

"How about a drink?" (I've been giving all day - here I can get something back.)

"Oops, dinner's burning. Get it yourself!" (No change out of this sucker!)

"Uh-huh!" (What a relief- she's stopped talking!)

The message to both reads: "Intimacy is impossible/ too difficult/ not worth it in this place. I will get it more cheaply somewhere else."

Neither partner is willing to take the risk of initiating intimacy through being vulnerable, because these coded messages convey that it is too dangerous. His already brittle self-concept could not bear another rejection, so he keeps his armour on. We will look in more detail at the nature of this armour in the next chapter.

CHANGING NEGATIVE ATTITUDES

Negative attitudes, particularly toward myself, have a negative impact on marriage. But I can change my self-concept by a process of affirmation, that is speaking about myself in a positive way. Just as the downward spiral of negative talk leading to a negative self-concept, negative behaviour and more negative talk, has had an impact on our lives, we can use these same forces in reverse for positive change.

We hung a poster in my daughter's bedroom of a grubby, mischievous little boy with a huge grin, emblazoned in large capitals with the words, "I KNOW I'M SOMEBODY- 'COS GOD DON'T MAKE NO JUNK!" Affirmation must be based on reality or truth to be believable. And the truth is that we are made in the image of God. We are more valuable in his economy than all the wealth in the universe. The events of the cross demonstrate God's price-tag on our lives. Having responded to the good news, let us believe and affirm our worth. Let us talk about ourselves in ways that reflect the reality of who we are in Christ. And let us affirm these same things about our partners. Replace the words "I'm no good", "I'm useless", "I'll never amount to anything" with "I'm precious", "I'm the apple of God's eye", "I'm a King's kid".

And let these affirmations be borne out by our behaviour. When it comes to the second part of healthy self-esteem, namely "I am competent", keep in mind that valuable is as valuable does. A good way to begin is to set five daily goals that stretch you, are personally worthwhile, attainable and specific.

My most successful day in sales coincided with the beginning of the habit of daily goal-setting. I had been procrastinating on a few tasks. Every morning when I went into my study to pick up my briefcase for work, my eyes fell on an in-tray piled 40 cm high with unfinished tasks. I left home feeling worthless and defeated, and it showed in my selling results. When I got home, the basket of rebuke stared me in the eye again and had further negative effects on my emotional presence with my family. The day I began setting daily goals, I listed the eight tasks in that basket and decided that I would finish two each day when I got home before going in to connect with the family or watch television. That day I got home, sat down at my desk, pulled the in-tray towards me and got to work. I became so immersed in the tasks that I had supper at the desk and worked late into the night. At 2:30 a.m. the next morning I completed the last task in the basket. I fell into bed, and got up at 6 a.m. to start my day.

Although I should have been low in energy that day, it seemed as though I attracted success. Selling was easy. I closed two deals that set a record in that company. People liked me. I liked me. And when I got home, my family also sensed that I was much nicer to have around. Even the dog was friendlier than usual! Why? Because my behaviour underscored my words. "I am competent" was the echo to "I am loved".

Everyone deserves to be able to feel that way about themselves, every day of their lives. Several marriages I have been involved with, through counselling, have been threatened by precisely the lack of self-esteem we have been discussing. This is especially true of spouses who have paused their careers to be stay-at-home parents, or of those who are building up a toxic level of cognitive dissonance as I described earlier. Depression, loss of motivation to work at the marriage, a general lack of interest in life and resulting marital difficulties that have no apparent external cause, are symptoms of these conditions. A systematic programme of goal-setting and planning for a healthy work/life balance invariably restores motivation and renews self-esteem. We will discuss this more in chapter 5. A spouse with a healthy self-image is able to give and receive love so that the marriage becomes fulfilling for both spouses.

When we make positive statements about ourselves that echo the reality of our faith, and back these statements up with deliberate action through daily goal-setting and achievement, we reverse the process of negative conditioning in our lives. This does not happen in an instant, but we will be surprised to see how quickly we will enjoy the benefits! I have seen people raised out of the trough of depression and self-doubt over one single weekend of taking the steps I have suggested.

Let God's opinion of you be your mirror and reflect those same thoughts to your spouse. Echo them in your behaviour. Let the accumulation of this positive input provide you with a new level of "want to", for a fulfilling life and marriage.

Chapter Three

CLEARING THE GROUND

A young boy walked past a vacant lot on his way to and from school. He was an industrious child and a keen gardener, so he traced the owner and asked his permission to use the piece of ground to grow flowers and vegetables. The owner agreed, and the youngster could be found there every day after school and every weekend, clearing rocks, digging and weeding, planting seeds, watering and fertilizing, until he had a fine crop of vegetables and flowers. One day he was sitting on the wall, watering his garden, when an elderly man walked by. "Who grew those flowers, son?" the old man asked.

"I did, sir," he replied.

"No, son, not you - God grew them."

The boy thought for a moment. "Yes, that's true," he said, "but you should have seen this place when God had it all to himself!"

I am sometimes asked why God allows things like an unhappy marriage to befall Christians. Doesn't our faith immunise us against things like divorce? At least a part of the answer is that becoming a Christian is the beginning, not the end, of a process of change. Perhaps the boy in our story confused the players, but the point is well taken. Weeds, rocks, flowers, vegetables and garbage are jumbled together in our lives. Leaving my mind uncultivated and merely trusting, or even praying, that my life will be happy and successful simply because I am a believer, or one of the "good guys", is a recipe for disillusionment. The good guys still have plenty of work to do!

As we pursue the model of change and growth discussed in chapter 2, it becomes clear that the way we think affects how we feel and determines our behaviour. Paul said: " ... do not be conformed to (the system of) this world, but be transformed by the renewing of your mind ... " (Romans 12:2). Our minds need to be made new through affirmation and thinking about ourselves in objective, realistic ways rather than negative, conditioned ones.

UNRESOLVED CONFLICTS

Experiments done in the 1950s and 1960s by researchers like Dr. Wilder Penfield bear consideration here.[18] Through electrical stimulation of different parts of the brain, he discovered that we store in minute detail every memory of every event we have ever paid attention to.[19] The emotions attached to those memories are in fact relived in our subconscious and cause certain emotional patterns to develop. Other researchers have written at length about the influence exerted on the current thinking, feeling, decision making and behaviour of adults by the secret inner "child".[20] The presence of this child in us creates the very real possibility of conflict in our lives as child and adult thoughts and feelings clash. Let me try to illustrate this process by sharing events from the lives of a couple I counselled.

> Janet was raised in a home where her father occasionally abused her and her siblings and even her mother. In her

---

[18] Wilder Penfield, *"Memory Mechanisms"*, Archives of Neurology and Psychiatry (No. 67, 1952), pp. 178 - 198.

[19] Wilder Penfield and H. H. Jasper, *Epilepsy and Functional Anatomy of the Human Brain* (London: Churchill Press, 1959), chapter 11.

[20] Harris, T.A. *I'm O.K., You're O.K.*. London: Jonathan Cape. 1973.

earliest memory of this, her father arrived home from "work" after dark. He smelt of alcohol when she greeted him at the door, and his raised voice preceded the onset of violence. She also remembers later occasions when she realized that it was dark and daddy wasn't home yet. She knew what was coming, and if she smelt that he had been drinking or heard him raise his voice, she slipped upstairs and hid under her bed to avoid the violence rather than wait for it. And it worked. The others may have borne the abuse, but she protected herself.

Janet is now twenty-five, happily married to Pete. One night Pete works late to complete an important contract and has a celebratory drink with his boss before leaving the office. He arrives home with flowers and chocolates, expecting a wonderful evening of intimacy and celebration with his wife. Janet meets him at the door. It is dark outside. As she kisses him, she smells the alcohol. She seems to freeze at his touch and does not even see the flowers or the chocolates. She tells him to get his own dinner - she is really tired and has a headache. She disappears to the bedroom, gets into bed, turns out the light and pretends to be asleep when he looks in on her. Pete spends the evening watching television alone, puzzled and hurt by her behaviour. A conflictual situation begins that is addressed only much later, the delay seriously damaging their marriage.

Are the two situations alike? Not at all. Pete's celebratory glass of bubbly and Janet's father's nights of drunkenness have very little in common. The reason why Pete got home late is very different from the reason her father came home late. But Janet's subconscious memory does not think about that rationally. Despite the reasons she gives for her behaviour, every similar situation involving old memories will very likely trigger a feeling of hurt in Pete, which, unless it is resolved, will turn to resentment and the further growth of weeds in his mind. I am not suggesting that Pete is blameless. The point is that

> Janet's past has a great deal more to do with the episode than his behaviour. Janet is not responding from the perspective of current reality and her adult rationality, but from memory, post-traumatic stress and childhood defensive habits.

We will discuss the necessity, forms and styles of communication in a later chapter, but in my counselling experience, many marriage partners who experience similar difficulties to Janet's, grew up in non-communicative or dysfunctional families and therefore did not learn to express their feelings to any depth. They are often married to spouses who on the other hand, may have come from warm, emotionally demonstrative families. Isn't it amazing how opposites attract each other? The one's expressiveness might draw the other one out, but later frustration will result from the inability and unwillingness of the incommunicative partner to talk. Their diverse backgrounds will create expectations that will probably not be met, and often not be talked about, until the couple has experienced considerable marital conflict.

A disastrous wedding night when sex was painful or humiliating; an argument about money that leaves one of the partners feeling degraded; years of unfulfilled expectations about communication; or, as in Janet's case, painful childhood experiences that leave one emotionally vulnerable and unable to cope with conflict - there are situations like these in every marriage. The issues are often unresolved or dealt with ineffectively. Some of the weeds may have been broken off at the surface so that the roots are left submerged. The garbage may have been buried for the moment... which reminds me...

Property developers in California in the 1960s discovered that it is impossible to bury car tyres permanently, when they built houses on land that had been reclaimed by covering landfills with topsoil and compacting it. When there were car tyres in the old landfill, months or even years later, the tyres would suddenly push up through the surface, uprooting lawns, shrubs or prize rosebushes in the process. The science confirmed that it is impossible to bury a cylindrical rubber object, as the pressure from below will always exceed the pressure from above, and it will eventually work its way to the surface. Unresolved conflicts from the past are like those tyres. You cannot bury feelings alive. You can repress them quite successfully for a while, but they will surface when you least expect them, in ways that will surprise you and cause further pain to all concerned.

How can we deal with these past causes of conflict, individually and as a married couple?

The past is a collection of memories, but specifically memories of failure. We have all been hurt or let down to some extent by those responsible for our upbringing. We have also let ourselves down. And our marriage partners have, to a greater or lesser extent, failed or injured us. If these hurts are left unresolved, they will not only prevent intimacy in our marriage, but will produce further conflict in the future. Couples argue more about past, unresolved conflicts than about new issues that arise in their marriage. How can we deal with this failure?

CONFLICT RESOLUTION

A woman who was not particularly attractive went to a well-known artist to have her portrait painted. At the unveiling of the finished portrait, when she saw it, she was greatly upset and said to the artist: "But I don't think it does me justice!" He replied: "Madam, what you need is not justice, but mercy!"

These words, mercy and justice, represent two ways of dealing with failure. Justice involves making the offender pay for his failure. Mercy is the decision of the offended one to pay for the offence himself, and thereby forgive or set the offender free.

Think about your situation. What are the things you remember from the past that cause frequent conflict within you in the form of guilt, anger or frustration, or that may have a bearing on the current conflicts in your marriage? Conflict resolution begins with an accurate description of the problem. Possible causes of conflict are needs that have been frustrated or neglected by my partner, unfulfilled expectations, hurt caused by the other's behaviour or neglect, or even past failed attempts at conflict resolution. I have counselled many couples whose marriages are filled with unspoken resentment, caused by the way one of them has dealt with an area of conflict. The offender is often blissfully unaware that his actions were hurtful and may even feel that he has resolved the conflict successfully, because there is no external sign that anything is wrong. Yet the hurt smoulders in his partner's heart, waiting for the moment when it will burst into unexpected, violent flame. The path to God's peace in your marriage begins with an evaluation of the present "state of the union", against the background of possible old, unresolved causes of conflict. List these issues and record your current feelings about each. Next, set aside a specific, regular time over the next few days or weeks, to talk about them. I suggest that initially you set a maximum of two such sessions per week, to avoid all your communication focusing on negatives that can be destructive and demotivating. Limit these sessions to 40 minutes each, for the same reason. Once the ground has been cleared, one discussion a week is sufficient to keep current with each other. This is essential if we are to prevent anger (a legitimate emotion) from becoming resentment or aggression, which are both destructive reactions to what started as a legitimate emotion.

Another firm rule that I have found helpful in the area of conflict resolution is that each partner has the right to call "time-out" when they need a breather. There is the danger that a time-out can become a cop-out. It is therefore important that the partner who calls the time-out must specify a time when the discussion can be resumed. Use the time-out to go aside and get in touch with your feelings, go for a walk, relax and review. Define them as clearly as you can, so that you are better equipped to disclose them when you come together again to talk. Here a couple shares how this rule helped them resolve conflict in their relationship:

> Your suggestion of calling "time-out" when one of us feels the need, especially if voices are raised or emotions are vented rather than expressed, is another very practical tool for maintaining intimacy in our marriage. We use the "time-out" to record our feelings in a journal and seek clarity. We come together again, at a time agreed on to express those feelings in a business-like environment, i.e. around the table, with full eye contact. This has created an environment for loving acceptance. The mere fact that both partners are committed to engaging in conflict resolution with care and consideration for one another is a means of healing.

Conflict is like dynamite -you can use it either to destroy a building; or to blow a hole through a mountain for the construction of a road. Couples testify that simply setting this process in motion invariably brings them closer together. The same couple added:

> Dealing with unresolved conflicts as you taught us to do, has been a healing agent in my life and my marriage. Learning to express my feelings rather than attack John, helped create an environment for him to listen and respond to me without blocking further communication through intimidation. Resolving an area of conflict is like removing a brick from the wall between us, so that the light begins to show through. The more bricks we pull down, the brighter the light and the smaller the obstacle between us in our day-to-day living. I feel freer to communicate without hidden meanings.

The diagrams below, adapted from Jay E. Adams' Guidelines for Conflict Resolution, illustrate how a problem (P), coming between two people (A and B) can cause either destructive conflict where they attack one another because of the problem; or constructive conflict where they join their energies to deal with the mutual enemy together.[21]

[21] Jay E. Adams, Christian Living in the Home (Grand Rapids: Baker Book House, 1972), pp.34 - 35.

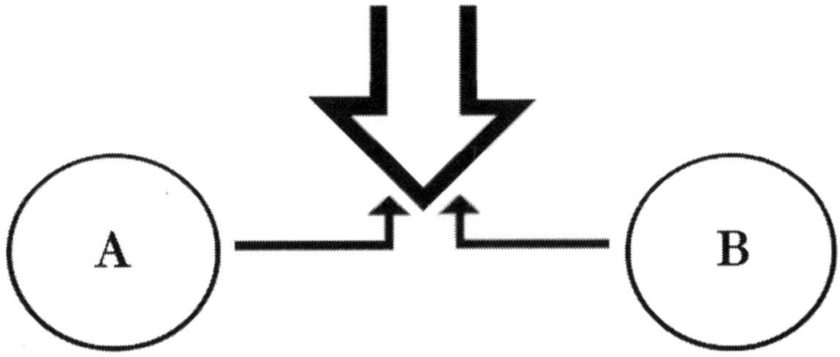

What is required to make conflict a constructive factor in a relationship? To get the two arrows to point in the same direction requires that one or both of the partners has the humility to accept responsibility and to say: "I understand. I'm sorry for my part in this. How can I help you?" and then to focus their attention on the problem. "A gentle answer deflects anger..."[22] is eminently practical

[22] Proverbs 15: 1 NLT

wisdom in circumstances like these. Jesus instructed his disciples to, "Agree with your adversary quickly, while you are on the way [to court] with him ... " (Matthew 5:25). That is to say: find a point of agreement before you focus on the point of disagreement. This is another illustration of what I call constructive conflict. Conflict can only be constructive when one party agrees with the other so that they can go in the same direction. It then becomes possible to focus on the real source of tension.

Once you have identified the cause of conflict and set a specific time to deal with it, begin the process. I call these sessions "table talk", because I suggest that you sit at a table for these discussions. A setting like this underscores the idea that you mean business, and that conflict resolution is a serious matter demanding a specific appointment in your week.

1. Take turns to raise items for discussion. Mention the issue you have identified, as well as your current feelings about it.

2. Use "I" messages in which you take responsibility for your feelings and resist the temptation to turn these into "you" messages that attack or apportion blame.

3. Be careful of disguised "you" messages, e.g. those that begin with "I feel that ... ". The addition of the word "that" implies that you are not stating a feeling but an opinion or a judgment. Variations of the "I" message may begin with the words "It is my perception ... " or "What I'm hearing you say is..." This kind of statement indicates to your partner that you are open to correction or guidance.

4. While your partner is sharing his feelings and thoughts about the issue at hand, your role is to actively listen, engaging with the one speaking with facial expressions, encouragement and, when appropriate, giving feedback to ask for and gain clarity. This enables you to establish whether you are listening

accurately, because it offers the speaker the opportunity to correct or adjust either his transmission or your reception of the message. True listening has only occurred when the listener can restate accurately both the content, and the feeling of what the speaker has communicated with him.

5. When the first speaker has done steps 1-3 above, the second one does the same, stating their perception, opinions and feelings about the same issue, inviting feedback and correction as per point 5.

This can be and usually is such a constructive exercise. Most of us sense that we are not being heard, particularly with regard to our feelings about issues. As Paul Tournier says, most communication today is a "dialogue of the deaf":

> Listen to all the conversations of the world... They are for the most part dialogues of the deaf. Each one speaks primarily in order to set forth his or her views, in order to justify himself or herself and accuse others. Exceedingly few exchanges of viewpoint manifest a real desire to understand the other person.[23]

Once you have raised and clarified an issue, three options arise as to how you might clear the ground, or resolve the conflict. These are: *forgiveness, negotiation towards agreement* and *the healing of emotions.* The first way, forgiveness, is the simplest and the most desirable way of dealing with the problem.

FORGIVENESS

We said that forgiveness can only take place once the offence has been clearly stated and understood by both parties. You may have discovered a nasty-looking, smelly or even dangerous object in your

[23] Paul Tournier, To Understand Each Other (Atlanta: John Knox Press, 1962), pp. 8 - 9.

plot of ground. It is vital that both you and your partner acknowledge its existence honestly. Name the failure you want to deal with clearly and openly. If you are the offender, ask your partner to forgive you. If you are the offended partner, you need to grasp a very important truth: *forgiveness is a decision that becomes a process.*

You and you alone can decide to forgive someone. Your decision will perhaps not immediately be accompanied by feelings of forgiveness, but it sets the process in motion. A range of varying and even startling emotions will usually follow.

From her studies of terminally ill patients, Dr Elizabeth Kübler-Ross identified five stages in the process of coming to terms with death, also known as the Grief Process.[24] These stages can be detected to varying degrees in any process of dealing with trauma or loss in our lives. I have seen them in those who are dying, and in their grieving relatives; in both parties involved in a divorce; in those recovering from major trauma, surgery or serious illness; and in virtually all cases where people have had to adjust emotionally to a new, stressful perception of themselves or experience of life. These five stages also occur in the process of "realising" forgiveness, so that we can speak of a ''forgiveness cycle".

The 5 stages Dr Kübler-Ross identified are ***Denial, Anger, Bargaining, Depression*** and ***Acceptance***. These do not usually flow easily and predictably from one to five. There is a degree of erratic movement from, for instance, denial to anger, to bargaining, back to anger, bargaining, depression, anger again, and so on.

It is important to realize this because we often feel that a second or third bout of the anger we believed we had dealt with, is an indication of unforgiveness. It is rather a sign that we are still in the process of realising, or coming to terms emotionally with, forgiving. We need to be patient with ourselves because, erratic as the process may be, it is a process, and we will eventually arrive at a point of

---

[24] Dr Elizabeth Kubler-Ross, On Death and Dying (New York: Macmillan, 1969), chapters 3 - 7.

acceptance. In extreme cases it can take up to two years to complete the process.

Let us look more closely at each of these five stages in the specific context of the process of forgiveness:

In the first stage, ***Denial***, the person who is forgiving the other may be fairly superficial in his view of what has happened. He tries to avoid discussion of the topic, and plays down any suggestion of offence on his part. He may say "I'm good – it's water off a duck's back!" or use biblical texts such as, "He who is without sin among you, let him throw a stone at her first"; or "all sin is the same", in an attempt to reduce the rising anger that he does not want to feel or admit to feeling.

In stage 2 the reality of the feelings of ***Anger*** become too insistent to deny, and the person finds himself unable to pretend any longer. Anger is hard to admit to, especially when we have held up our forgiveness as a badge of merit. In addition, most of us are unskilled at expressing anger in reasonable ways. The most common models for expressing anger with which we have grown up, are bitterness and rage. It may at first express itself as general irritability, sulking or "the silent treatment", but may explode as verbal or even physical outbursts of rage from time to time, whether against the person that is seen as an offender, or at God, or at life in general, or at the nearest person or object in the way. This stage is usually accompanied by guilt and a sense of failure.

> A couple I was counselling after a near divorce because of the husband's infidelity, were both puzzled by the fact that the wife had recurring feelings of anger, even though she had decided to forgive her husband. He was starting to react to her anger with some of his own, and was uncertain about how to love her. Understanding the cycle of forgiveness helped them to be patient. He was able to pay the price of self-denial by simply holding her when she felt angry. Those times of just holding one another had the effect of restoring her trust in

him. In this way her anger was used to bring them together rather than drive them apart.

Of course, there is more than this one aspect to the process. It requires work, love and commitment from both partners, but the decision to love each other through the negative times is crucial to the successful completion of the cycle.

Stage 3, the ***Bargaining*** stage, is a defence mechanism used to reduce or deflect the feelings of anger. It involves the attempt to exact some form of emotional payment from the offender or to get them or God to make the offended party feel better. Bargaining can take the form of manipulative demands, for example: "God, if you answer this prayer, I promise I'll go to church every Sunday / give money to the church / read my Bible / quit smoking…" "I'll forgive and forget if: you change your job/ we can move in with my parents / we can go to a new church." Bargaining can be more or less subtle, but usually involves spoken or unspoken pressure on one partner or the other requiring change of behaviour of the other in exchange for privileges.

A man was late for an appointment, and was looking for a space in a parking lot, then remembered and did what his wife usually did – prayed for God's help. He said: "God, if you find me a parking space NOW, I'll go to church every Sunday. Twice every Sunday. And I'll tithe on my gross income. And give $1000 to the Church Building Fund!" As he said the last thing, he saw a parking space, and then added: "Don't worry, God – cancel that – I found it by myself!"

Stage 4, ***Depression***, is one of our societies' current scourges. It is responsible for physical conditions like headaches, digestive issues and arthritis, and interpersonal problems at home or at work, and can be of fleeting duration or gain a chronic stranglehold on your life. It takes many forms, from a deep sense of despair or hopelessness, grief, isolation, phobias and often, self-harm or suicide.

The comedian Steven Wright said "Depression is merely anger without enthusiasm."[25] Although that sounds funny, I believe there

[25]https://best-quotations.com/authquotes.php?auth=1031

is a sad truth behind it, and that depression is actually anger turned in on oneself, and in terms of this grief process, if we neglect to deal appropriately with the Anger stage, we will pay that bill in the form of deeper levels of Depression. The degree to which we feel the awful paralysis of depression in the process of forgiveness, is inversely proportionate to the degree to which we have expressed or dealt effectively with our anger.

The 5th and final stage of grief is ***Acceptance***. In this stage the person is emerging into a more forward-thinking, rational and hopeful way of being. He can accept that he and especially his emotions are normal. She has learned to express what she feels in appropriate ways and truly to accept the offender in the full light of the offence, with the warm, open-hearted recognition that the offence is past and "the sinner is separate from the sin". It is a stage accompanied by an ability to leave the past in the past, to see the offender through new eyes. Years ago, I heard a pastor explaining what the biblical word "justified" means. He quoted an old lawyer who explained it by saying "Why, it means that, after I've been 'justified', I have no record against me. It is 'just-(as)-if-I'd' never sinned!" This is a character-trait of a merciful God, who sees us as not only forgiven, but cleansed, without a black mark, without a record of wrongdoing.[26]

If the offended party lacks the information, emotional strength or self-acceptance to see this process of forgiveness through to the end, the resulting stalemate can destroy a relationship. On the other hand, the end of the process promises not just the erasure of negative emotions, but the onset of fresh positive ones. It doesn't just restore 'neutral' ground – it causes new levels of warmth and intimacy to arise between the partners. The safety valve and the key to conflict resolution and renewed intimacy through a patient working through of the cycle is open, honest communication of feelings. Tell your partner how you are feeling at each stage of the process. Learn a new language of "feeling-speak" so as to articulate emotion thoroughly

26 The Good News translation of 1 Corinthians 13:5 has it saying "love does not keep a record of wrongs".

and constructively. Learn to listen for not just what someone thinks, or what has caused offence, but how this makes them feel at the deepest level. The best analogy for this kind of communication is an onion. Someone wisely said, concerning life (and let me apply it here to relationship), that it is "…like an onion. You peel it away one layer at a time. And sometimes, you weep."

NEGOTIATION

As I said earlier, forgiveness may not always take place immediately, and the couple may need to clear the ground by negotiating their way to an agreement.

This process starts with the person who "owns the problem" or is most affected by it (usually the offended party), stating the cause of the conflict as they perceive it, describing their feelings about it, and suggesting a way of resolving the problem. During this phase, the other party should engage in active listening, offering feedback to ensure that the problem, with all its emotional ramifications, is clearly articulated and understood.

After this, the "offender" should respond, offering their thoughts, describing their feelings, and suggesting possible alternatives as to how to resolve the conflict. Again, the other party engages in active listening. This process should continue, each one speaking without interruption (unless with a clarifying question) and alternatively actively listening, until an agreement is reached.

This may simply mean a clear understanding by one partner of how they have offended the other, or it may be a joint strategy for dealing with the issue in the future. Often the very fact that communication has taken place is enough to produce resolution, reconciliation and renewed warmth and closeness between the partners. An extract from a letter I received bears this out:

> The ACTION of Jim in listening to me generates incredible warmth towards him. I feel closer to him, more intimate and

> more whole. J feel, for the first time in eight years of marriage, loved and accepted. I feel as though he has been, for me, "God with skin".[27]

If neither forgiveness nor a negotiation towards agreement takes place initially, more time, allowing for the grief process described above, might be required. Respect your own, and one another's, emotions, and allow them time to heal.

EMOTIONAL HEALING

Many of us live with damaged emotions, often the result of neglect, deprivation or abuse in childhood when we had no emotional defence mechanisms with which to protect ourselves from such hurt. I know people who were so abused in childhood that, even as Christian adults of some standing, they are incapable of emotional warmth. Sinful patterns of behaviour may be established in an attempt to reduce the pain. For example, women who, as young girls, were abused by their fathers, are likely to grow up with some antagonism, whether overt or covert, towards all men. Men who grew up with domineering or manipulative mothers, may grow up with an excessive sense of obligation towards them, or with resentment towards all women, including their wives.

There are endless pain-producing factors in our backgrounds. The need for emotional healing is revealed by an inability to respond appropriately to others, or recurring patterns of emotional-relational dysfunction. We need to face and understand the subconscious basis for inappropriate emotional responses. This usually involves reliving the memory of the painful experience with a trusted person

[27] Here she was quoting a story I usually tell in my seminars, where a child woke up in the middle of the night, crying. Her mother went to her and soothed her fears and prayed with her until she had stopped crying. The mom got up to leave the child's room, but her daughter said "NO! Stay with me!" The mother replied "It will be fine. We've prayed, and asked God to stay with you. He's right here!" But the little girl said, through new tears "RIGHT NOW, I NEED GOD WITH SKIN ON!"

listening, and inviting God's healing presence into that space. There are resources available for all of us in the form of counsellors, seminars, books, retreat centres and caring friends. Talk to someone, ask questions, research sources of help, and be sure to get help when the situation is beyond "self-help". Don't allow a painful past to define or control you in the present or the future.

The promise of God is that those who come to him for healing will not be disappointed. We can be transformed by the renewing of our minds. The healing of damaged emotions does not mean that we will never again experience feelings of rejection, fear, anger, resentment, or whatever our habitual response was. It does, on the other hand, mean that we will be free to choose again. We will be free to say "no" to fear and "yes" to risk-taking, "no" to resentment and "yes" to love. We will be free to communicate rather than remaining in emotional isolation. Every time we act on that freedom, we reinforce a new habit, and that habit will eventually become a new lifestyle. When we resolve old or new conflicts in constructive ways, we are engaging in the task the young lad in our opening story undertook. We are clearing the ground and thereby making possible the planting, fertilizing and maturing of productive, life-enhancing "plants" in our lives. We are making ourselves candidates for real intimacy in our marriages by becoming whole, transparent, loving people who are not always on the defensive.

Chapter Four

OF HEADS AND HEARTS AND THINKING CAPS

Intimacy of the kind we are discussing, pre-supposes two equal yet different people moving towards each other, without fear or dishonesty and meeting on the level ground of mutual acceptance, transparency and active listening. The shocking fact is that often, the greatest hindrance to this happening effectively, is the form of Christianity that many Christian teachers apply to marriage.

ROLES

Most of the teaching about Christian marriage that I have been exposed to, focuses on the *roles* that the Bible expects, instructs or commands husbands and wives to play in marriage. One of the best-known verses, and the one least appreciated by women, on the subject of how wives should relate to their husbands, tells wives to "submit to" their husbands, "as to the Lord" (Ephesians 5 :22). Other verses in the same chapter seem to reinforce this concept, speaking of the husband as the "head of the wife, as also Christ is head of the church" (verse 23). In 1 Corinthians 11, Paul says the same thing, declaring that "the head of woman is man" (verse 3) and that the "woman is the glory of man" (verse 7).

Verses like these, especially if they are taken out of their biblical and cultural context, create the impression of an "over/under" or "superior/inferior" relationship between husbands and wives. Or worse, they become ammunition for husbands to use on their wives, who in turn accumulate other, seemingly contradictory verses with which to defend themselves: "But the Bible says you have to love me as Christ loved the church, buster, so get your bit right before you tell me what to do!"

This situation can easily deteriorate into a state of domestic warfare, with each partner using manipulative weapons (e.g. withholding sex!) to enforce Biblical observance! This is like two boys wanting to play a game. One owns the bat, the other the ball. When things do not go as he wants them to, the one says: "If you don't let me bat first, I'm taking my ball and going home!" The other replies in kind: "If you don't let ME bat first, I'm taking my bat and leaving!"

How tragic that we miss the point of the Bible's message by such a margin! But even more tragic that we put the blame for our folly on God Himself! The law of the "new covenant" is the law of love. We will discuss in the next chapter the kinds of love the Bible requires of us as marriage partners, but we should see the "fine print" (the instructions, commands and moral requirements) of the New Testament as elaborations of the law of love. When the very words of the New Testament become weapons to destroy the possibility of God's kind of love, something is wrong with the way we are using them.

As Westerners, we tend to find our identity in the role we fulfil. We also impose that identity on every area in which we operate, like the medical doctor who was trying to fix his friend's car, telling his friend "Trust me – I'm a doctor!" When we are introduced to someone, "What do you do?" is the next question after "How do you do?". The answer to the question is, in fact, more important to us than almost anything else. In this way I become, in other people's eyes and usually in my own too, a collection of roles. I am a pastor, a lecturer, a counsellor, a Life Coach, a Sales Executive.

There - now you know me! Will you know me better if l explain these roles to you? You may know some of the things I *do*, but if I were your husband, would that knowledge ensure happiness, love and intimacy between us?

I sometimes smile when I see our local handyman driving by. The name of his business is painted on the side of his van - **Hire-a-Husband**. It conjures up all kinds of images. I wonder if, in addition to the usual toolbox, he also has in the van a box of toys for the children to play with, a first-aid kit, skeleton keys to lock any house, baby food to do the midnight shift ...the mind boggles!

RESULTS OF THESE ROLES

The model of marriage that is implied by these role definitions is the Functional Marriage Model. It conveys the understanding that each member of the family is like a part of a machine. As long as each part performs its function, the machine will operate smoothly. Functionality buys harmony, and ensures happiness for all.

Thus, based on a superficial reading of Ephesians and Corinthians, with a dollop of 1st Peter, a good wife is one who submits to her husband. Her role is to see to his wellbeing, provide him with sex, cook his meals, sing his praises, bear his children, and crown him king. A good husband is one who brings home the bacon, provides a pleasant home in the right suburb, holds a good position at work and in the church, disciplines the children when they are naughty, makes the decisions about money, careers ("No wife of mine will ever work"), holidays, church membership, and so on. I have even heard pastors say that a wife has no direct accountability to God, but is spiritually accountable only to and through her husband. He in turn must answer to God for his and her spiritual state and behaviour!

Husbands who believe this interpretation of the New Testament, attempt to exercise an autocratic headship over their homes. In fact, they understand the word "head" from a cultural perspective. To them, being the head, means to be the *boss* or *chief.* The word has associations with *head*master, *head*man, managing director, president or king. This kind of husband might delegate some authority to his wife, usually over the children and their upbringing, schooling, feeding, entertainment, transportation and discipline. He wants to see them only when they are bathed and fed, neatly clothed, quiet and obedient. His concern with them is that they make him feel and look good in the community, the church, the sports field and the PTA.

Our concern in this book is *intimacy* in marriage, and it is in this regard that the role-related or functional marriage concept is most destructive. When roles create an over/under style of relationship between husband and wife, real communication is blocked. The husband is filling the role either of a monarch or a parent when he succeeds in implementing this model. One does not express opinion, let alone *self-disclose* to a monarch, and there is no question of a monarch discussing his feelings with a serf! Parents, likewise, do not tell their children how they feel - only what, when, where and how to do what the parent requires. When the child asks the parent, "Why?", the answer is usually "Because I said so!"

When this model is imported into a marriage, the wife is seen as "less", as a Child to her husband's Parent, not allowed an opinion, or the right to question his. Her emotional condition is usually one of passive aggression. She might comply for a time because this is the least painful option, much as a child will comply with the wishes of a parent who intimidates them. Her real or imagined dependence on her husband, in the child-bearing and child-rearing years, will increase this trend to compliance. But I believe one of the reasons why so many marriages fail after the couple's children grow up and leave home, is that the wife then feels the freedom to make her stand. She says "So far and no further!" The resulting explosion is often a great shock to her husband, because he believed all along that his wife enjoyed being a subservient nobody.

A man came to see me when this happened in his marriage. The family had long been part of a church that made the harsh application of the Scriptures to the marriage relationship as I described above. He was in fact a leader in that church. Suddenly, when the empty nest stage happened, his wife told him enough was enough. His words to me were: "My wife has become demonised! Can you exorcise her?" I told him no such thing had occurred. What she had done was decide to grow up, and he should wake up!

THE CURSE

The Old Testament, and specifically the book of Genesis, teaches us that the result of "the fall of humanity" was an arrangement of relationships between men, women and creation that is called "the curse" (Genesis 3: 14 - 19).

It may sound harsh, but I believe that the curse was part of God's mercy. It left the humans in a relationship of tension with the world and one another so that they would be forced to seek relief, direction and peace from God. Adam is told: "In toil you shall eat ... the herbs of the field. In the sweat of your face you shall eat bread ... " (verses 17 - 19). The curse on Adam is that he will have to be macho if he is to survive! The woman is told she would in future have pain in childbirth: "In pain you shall bring forth children; Your desire shall be for your husband, And (yet) he shall rule (harshly) over you" (verse 16, parentheses mine). Her curse is the desire for, and dependence on, this harsh man who will help her fulfil her desire to bear children. This desire will be fulfilled only through great agony. She will need as well as desire her husband, but his survival mechanism will be brought into their relationship, so that he will "rule" over her with harshness.

Understand that this arrangement called "the Curse" was never God's ideal, but a remedial arrangement to curb the runaway tendency to self-salvation and entitlement in the human race, for whom God desired a trusting, vulnerable, intimate relationship with Himself and one another. The weariness of toil against an adverse environment, and the pain and stress of love against the background of co-dependency, were all meant to show humans their need of God's empowering Grace.

The curse created a dynamic tension between all concerned, and sowed in the human race and in marriage the seeds of harsh rulership or autocracy on the part of men and dependent, dutiful subservience or passive aggression on the part of women. Old Testament society abounded with examples of this kind of marriage relationship. However, we need to remember that this was not the normative state for humanity and our relationships. It is rather to be seen as a corrective. The breach of relationship with God and His ways (peace, love and justice) results in a loss of those ways between His creatures. The rest of the Bible is the story of God calling us back, saying "Are you sick and tired of it yet? Do you want to get back to a place of peace, love and justice? Come home to me, and I'll restore you to that place."

Why, then, would the gospel, as it is applied by Paul to marriage, simply teach and enforce the same, negative, conflict-ridden rules of relationship that were implicit in the curse? Imagine an oppressed, Jewish-Christian woman in Ephesus in 60AD, coming to church to hear this exposition of the good news just received from the hand of Paul. The preacher expounds on Paul's letter and reaches the conclusions highlighted early in this chapter. I can hear Mrs Cohen say to Mrs Levy: *"For vot do I need more reasons to be a nobody in my home? Let's leave now, darling, already there's enough sadness!"*

THE GOOD NEWS

I do not believe that the gospel was ever intended to convey the idea of dutiful subservience on the part of women. I am convinced that Paul's call to submission is intended to reverse the curse and its symptoms. Let me explain what I mean:

HEADSHIP AND SUBMISSION

Paul begins his teaching on relationships, addressed to all Christians: husbands, wives, parents, children, ministers and lay persons, with a blanket statement: " ...*submitting to one another* out of reverence for

Christ." (Ephesians 5 :21 NLT, emphasis mine). The word "submit" comes from the Greek word *hupotasso*. It means to "arrange under". It is important to notice that this is an active verb. It conveys the action of someone "submitting themself". It is not a passive verb, where something is done *to* you or *enforced*, but implies a choice, an act of the will. In Paul's usage of "hupotasso" he implies that it is something I do from my own free will, hence the King James Bible's rendition "*Submit yourselves* to one another…" I hope you can see from this little excursion into Greek grammar that anyone saying to another person *"You must submit to me…"* is abusing both good grammar and good understanding and usage of the Bible! Submission is only Biblical when I give it freely, out of love, to another.

> A little boy was jumping and playing around in the lounge where his father was trying to watch TV.
> "Johnny, sit down!" Said the dad.
> "I won't I" Replied Johnny.
> "Sit down!" repeated the father. "I won't!" said Johnny.
> Finally, the father got up, grabbed the boy and shoved him into a chair. "I said sit down!"
> Johnny glared up at him for a moment, then said, *"On the inside I'm still standing up!"*

Thus it is with anyone upon whom submission is enforced. The state of passive aggression that we spoke of earlier is the inevitable result of enforced compliance.

To return to Paul: In my view, the verses that follow his blanket instruction in verse 21 *("submit yourselves to one another")* spell out the details of this instruction. We are *all* to submit to one another. So how do husbands submit themselves to their wives, and how do wives submit to their husbands? How do parents submit to their children, and children to their parents? Even more radically, how do masters (employers) submit themselves to their servants (employees), and vice versa? Seeing that this is a book about marriage, I will apply the rule only to husbands and wives, and leave it to you to make the applications to the other relationships in your life.

THE SUBMISSION OF HUSBANDS

> *Ephesians 5:21 And further, submit to one another out of reverence for Christ…*
> *25 For husbands, this means love your wives, just as Christ loved the church. He gave up His life for her 26 to make her holy and clean, washed by the cleansing of God's word. 27 He did this to present her to Himself as a glorious church without a spot or wrinkle or any other blemish. Instead, she will be holy and without fault. 28 In the same way, husbands ought to love their wives as they love their own bodies. For a man who loves his wife actually shows love for himself. 29 No one hates his own body but feeds and cares for it, just as Christ cares for the church. 30 And we are members of his body. 31 As the Scriptures say, "A man leaves his father and mother and is joined to his wife, and the two are united into one." 32 This is a great mystery, but it is an illustration of the way Christ and the church are one. 33 So again I say, each man must love his wife as he loves himself, and the wife must respect her husband.*

I will start with husbands, because I believe the idea of "headship" referred to in the Scriptures quoted earlier, suggest that the initiative and responsibility for a mutually submissive family is theirs, in the same way that the action of my hand in picking up this coffee mug started in my brain ("head"!) Paul speaks of men as the "head", not in the sense of "boss", but in the sense of the place of initiative and coordination. I'll say more about this later.

In the case of husbands, Paul calls to mind the example of Christ. He says that they are to love their wives as Christ loved the church. Initiate a loving relationship by being loving! Keep in mind the outcomes of harsh control, toughness, "feel-no-pain", "cowboys-don't-cry" "machoness" that the curse put on the male human, to understand how radical the gospel really is!

Their love is to be sacrificial, vulnerable and self-giving (verse 25)

They are to be tender and caring (verse 29)

They are to be self-disclosing and affirming, "washing" and refreshing their wives with their words (verse 26)

They are to be nurturing and seek the wellbeing and full potential of their wives (vs 27)

If we see these instructions against the background of the curse, we find that Paul commands husbands to ***reverse the curse***, to relinquish their macho disposition when they come home, and to *submit themselves to tenderness*. This means that they fulfil their role not so much by *doing* certain jobs but by *being* imitators of Christ.

Listen to how Peter says this: (1 Peter 3:7):

> *In the same way, you husbands must give honour (preferential place) to your wives. Treat your wife with understanding (consideration) as you live together. She may be weaker than you are, but she is your equal partner in God's gift of new life. Treat her as you should so your prayers will not be hindered.* (NLT with my inserts)

The Bible says that Christ is the head of His Body, the Church. Christ is the head, not primarily in terms of being the king of a realm, but rather the head of a body. The head is responsible for the health, wellbeing and coordination of the parts of the body, so that the proper function of each part can be gladly offered.

As I said earlier, I have discussed husbands first because I believe the husband's responsibility is to be proactive as was Jesus. Can you imagine husbands taking the initiative in self-disclosure? In self-denial? In sacrificial self-giving? In "calling out" by affirmation and recognition the best in his wife, and serving that best with faith and energy? This could make for some exciting times of intimacy!

THE SUBMISSION OF WIVES

> *Ephesians 5:21 And further, submit to one another out of reverence for Christ.*
> *22 For wives, this means submit (yourselves) to your husbands as to the Lord. 23 For a husband is the head of His wife as Christ is the head of the church. 24 As the church submits to Christ, so you wives should submit to your husbands in everything.*

What is the specific outworking of submission for the wife? Women had been newly liberated by the gospel, in terms of their place before God, in the Church, and in marriage. The example Jesus lived, in His easy acceptance of women as equal to men in status, spiritual authority, leadership and ministry had resulted in this liberation expanding with the Church, first among Jews in the diaspora and second, among gentiles. The tendency of any oppressed person or group when liberation comes, is to overreact, seek retribution or take advantage of their new liberty and flaunt it in front of their former oppressors. I believe that in Ephesus, and in Corinth, this was happening in the form of an extreme and militant feminist cult.[28] Paul, in the Ephesian text, is urging women not to follow this over-reaction, or indeed any form of passive aggression, and tells them to use their freedom in Christ positively, and be vulnerable with their husbands in a way that is caring, gentle, non-defensive and co-operative. This is echoed in the first epistle of Peter (3:1-4):

> *In a similar way, you wives must submit yourselves to your husbands... 3 Your beauty should not be an external one... 4*

[28] See Derek Morphew, *Different But Equal* (Cape Town: Vineyard International Publishing, 2009) who expounds on this (Chapter 3) and shows how modern feminist theology is informed more by Gnosticism than the Biblical text. See also Dr. Lucy Peppiatt ***Rediscovering Scripture's Vision for Women: Fresh Perspectives on Disputed Texts.*** IVP Academic, 2019; ***Unveiling Paul's Women: Making Sense of 1 Corinthians 11:2-16.*** Eugene, Or.: Wipf and Stock, 2018; ***Women and Worship at Corinth: Paul's Rhetorical Arguments in 1 Corinthians.*** Eugene, Or.: Wipf and Stock. 2015.

> *Instead, it should be the inner disposition of the heart, consisting in the imperishable quality of a gentle and quiet spirit, which God values greatly.*

They are to submit to their husbands "as to the Lord" (verse 22). How does the church submit to Christ? Out of love rather than fear, out of faith rather than force, because of unconditional acceptance rather than performance-orientation. By wanting to please him out of love, not because they are terrified of his displeasure. Paul is saying to wives: "Replace the fear that used to motivate you in marriage with love that frees you to respond to your husband positively, gladly and with initiative. Seek to serve his wellbeing, his best life, his full potential, and see where that takes your relationship!"

MUTUAL ACCEPTANCE, MUTUAL HONOUR

The model of headship Paul calls to mind in 1 Corinthians 11, is that of the Father with regard to His Son Jesus Christ (verse 3). As Christians we would never suggest that this is an over/under-relationship, for Christ, as the Nicene Creed puts it, is "of the essence of the Father, God of God, Light of Light, very God of very God, begotten, not made…" in short, co-equal with the Father! Take a moment to let that sink in, and let it shape how we as married couples should view each other!

Here, in dealing with the question of the inter-relationship of husbands and wives, Paul makes a fundamental statement, saying "in the Lord", that is, as both marriage partners live out their relationship with Christ, they must realise that "neither is man independent of woman, nor woman independent of man" (verse 11). They are interdependent and co-equal, and their status is mutually derived from God (verse 12). The nature of God, who is love, is to be the source, the power and the gauge of our relationship as husband and wife. It is in this love that we are freed to give of ourselves in communication and mutual submission, acting for each other's wellbeing. How does this work in practice?

First, it enables us to see ourselves, not according to rank, but as willing servants of one another. Neither partner is the parent or the child of the other; each is given the dignity of equal status as a free and independent adult.[29]

Studies in both neuroscience and psychology revealed that within every human over the age of 6 years reside three co-existent "ego states", namely the Parent (a composite of all authority figures who have ever influenced us, especially in our first 6 years); the Child (a set of conditioned responses to the Parent); and the Adult (the rational, objective and responsible part which is both referee between the other two, and the mechanism for changing mindsets and psycho-social attitudes and getting us to maturity).

What is an adult? He is someone who has grown up, reached maturity and assumed responsibility for his own life. Adults are not only able to, but are intended to make their own decisions about their goals, dreams, preferences and lifestyles. They are also responsible for the consequences of their decisions. An adult is able to be objective, to stand at a distance from his thoughts and feelings, and does not simply allow his feelings to rule him. An adult is able to accept himself with his feelings. These feelings are not tyrants but servants, not rulers but indicators of their needs.

The Parent ego-state prompts us to authoritarian, prejudiced and nurturing attitudes and behaviour. When two people in parent-mode talk to one another, we observe a phenomenon called "the clash of experts". Each tries to "out-expert" the other, to tell a better story, to quote a higher authority, to be more convincing and therefore to win. They will often "play the man and not the ball" in this pursuit, and tend to put people and things in cubbyholes, which in turn allow a greater degree of control.

The inner Child is a memory file in the brain containing conditioned responses to the Parent. The Child is playful and imaginative but

[29] In what follows, I will be using the understanding of Transactional Analysis as described by Eric Berne, *Games People Play*. London: Penguin. 1964; and T.A. Harris, *I'm O.K., You're O.K.*. London: Jonathan Cape. 1973.

also adaptive and self-centred. When two children communicate, apart from imaginative games, if they disagree there is a similar phenomenon as that between two Parent types, but children do not have the courage or emotional resources to enforce their views. Their selfcentredness is awesome, but they usually have to resort to spite, bullying, manipulation or the intervention of parents to resolve a stalemate.

A parent can communicate with a child at certain levels, but the communication is of the "talk down" variety. Parents cannot employ logic or reason to persuade their children. They do not discuss issues with them but tell them what they expect or demand from them. The only weapons the child has for emotional survival are: manipulation through guilt, fear or procrastination; and compliance leading to survival but with a passive-aggressive attitude.

When two adults communicate, there is an underlying assumption of equality, mutual respect and dignity. Each assumes that the other has a right to his opinions, judgments, feelings and preferences. Persuasion, in the event of a disagreement, will take the form of producing facts, using reason and logic, disclosing feelings and pursuing an objective. They will not take responsibility for each other's feelings, but will accept them, make allowance for and respect them. When these two adults have to live together, such mutual respect will challenge them and give them security. The challenge is not one of having to establish *who* is right but *what* is right. Their security lies in knowing that in this place I am always accepted with dignity.

What kind of communication characterises your marriage? What kind would you like to see characterise it? I believe that life with a clone of myself would be boring. There have been times in my marriage when I wanted to make Lorraine think exactly as I do about everything. I won every argument (at least in my own eyes!) and, if a stalemate occurred, I tried to pull rank. What a hard act to sustain! Discovering the freedom of adult-to-adult communication and acceptance has led to a situation where I can celebrate my wife's uniqueness. There are areas in which we agree perfectly, others in which we are in a process of dialogue, and those on which we have agreed to disagree, agreeably!

There is a need, in all this, to distinguish between the non-negotiable (your values), the negotiable and important (high-priority items), and what is negotiable if we have the time (lowpriority issues).

For instance, one's spiritual allegiances as a Christian, are non-negotiable. It is difficult to have complete oneness with someone who is antagonistic to your faith. This would fall into the area of values.

Questions such as the way you use your leisure time, and where you will spend this Christmas (your folks or mine?), are high-priority negotiable issues. You need to employ the process of negotiation we outlined in chapter 3, to resolve this kind of question. The last category, low-priority negotiables, is one in which you need to travel light. Do not make issues of these. Guard against majoring on minors. And even when you do need to discuss how to squeeze the toothpaste, please maintain a sense of humour!

I have discovered that not only is loving and mutual acceptance easier on all concerned (including me), but it is also much more fun. And, of course, the resulting charm that is evident in me is much more appealing to my wife! Husbands, make this statement about yourselves every day: "I am responsible to seek and serve the wellbeing of every member of this family- my wife first!" Think about this when you are going to work. Think about it during your day. Very importantly, think about it on the way home and up the driveway. Think about it when you walk into the house tired - she is, too. Think about it when the supper needs to be cooked and when the children need bathing. Let it motivate you to run a bath for her, or to make her a cup of tea. Be an eager competitor in a race to win the "servant stakes", as Paul puts it in Romans 12:10 "Love each other with genuine affection, and take delight in honouring each other" (or "outdo one another in showing honour") [30]. Imagine

[30] Romans 12:10 ISV (and ESV)

a marriage relationship where the competition was to be the best at serving, honouring your spouse more than you do yourself - and then, make that dream a reality!

That is what I meant by the chapter title. Heads need thinking caps. Heads need to consider and be inventive in their motivation care and co-ordination of the body. This is the kind of headship that Jesus exemplified. It is the kind that seeks to serve. Love like this does not seek a reward- it is its own reward. Be careful not to do it on a quid pro quo basis, for your integrity's sake. It is your responsibility before God, it is what you promised when you made your wedding promises. However, if it does not produce a willing co-operation and loving responsiveness in your wife, I will eat your copy of this book!

Wives, a husband who lays down his weapons at the door, is a vulnerable man. You could really injure him if you wanted to, but you would be sabotaging peace and intimacy in the place where you need it most. Submission involves the willingness to respond with love to your husband. Seek to serve his wellbeing as a lifestyle of love. Resist every temptation to be competitive in your home. Take the initiative in all the aspects of intimacy that this book talks about: planning and goal-setting, self-disclosure and intimacy with regard to feelings and thoughts, climate creation and, very importantly, freedom in sexual intimacy.

It is important to re-emphasize that the particular responsibility of each co-equal partner in the kind of marriage we are talking about, is independent and unconditional. I am not called to love my wife *if* she submits to me, nor is she only to submit *if* I am the ideal husband. The commitment we make to mutual submission is "as to the Lord". As if Jesus were your husband. With your heart open and vulnerable to Him first.

There will be times when one of the partners will score a 2 or a 3 on being the husband, or wife, that God has called them to be. That is not the time for retributive withdrawal but for creative, loving engagement. In doing your part, you release God's energy into your marriage and, with general goodwill on both sides, you will usually see a corresponding energizing of your partner. However, difficult times do not excuse us from doing the Will of God. The biblical instructions we have talked about are stated in objective, eternal and viable terms and apply no matter what our circumstances may be, within reason and within the bounds of the Grace God gives.

By this, however, I do *not* mean to suggest, as some do, that a woman must put up with abuse because she is a Christian. Quite the contrary! Abuse is as much a covenant-breaker as is adultery, and only willing, co-operative, mutual honour qualifies anyone to have a marriage partner.

Chapter Five

IF YOU FAIL TO PLAN YOU PLAN TO FAIL

Most people enter marriage without any idea of what it will require of them, completely untrained and idealistic, believing that being in love will guarantee unending bliss.

In the marriage and divorce recovery seminars I teach, I usually find that on average 10% of the delegates had any kind of premarital training or counselling. And when I ask people why they got married or why they want to get married, the usual reply is: "Because we love each other". While this is sweet and hard to argue against, the fact is that we use the same word to describe why we chose our brand of car, or how we feel about our dog, ice cream or Italian food! And so often, and so easily, the couple who told me they wanted to marry because they love each other, within 5 years are seeking help or seeking divorce because "we no longer love each other"!

LOVE

Three Greek words used in the Greek New Testament are translated by our English word "love". They describe the different dimensions of love that are necessary if a marriage is to succeed. I think of them in terms of the three-legged, cast-iron pots we use in South Africa to cook our traditional *potjiekos* (pot food). These delicious stews can have simple or exotic ingredients, the recipe can be very scientific or rather haphazard, but no matter how wonderful these are, if one of the legs of the pot breaks off, the result will be a burnt, unappetizing mess spilt into the fire.

The first word, *agăpe*, describes a love that is unconditional and often undeserved. It can be best defined as "an unconditional commitment to an imperfect person". It shows itself in commitment or "stickability". It is not a feeling but a decision to act for the wellbeing of the one you love. It loves even the unlovely and unlovable. Most importantly, people do not naturally love in this way. This kind of love is the expression of God's nature. We only possess it to the measure that we receive it from him. We are called to love all people in this way- including our spouse.

The second word, *phileo*, describes brotherly affection or friendship. It enjoys the company of the one it loves, and manifests itself in shared time, energy, interests and goals. *Phileo* produces and is maintained by communication. We are to demonstrate *phileo* to all those we regard as friends - including our spouse.

The third word for love is *eros*, the root of words like "erotic". It describes sexual or romantic love and takes sensual delight in the appearance and sexuality of the person it loves. It seeks sensual expression through touch and physical closeness, and ultimately through sexual intercourse. According to Scripture it is meant to be expressed in this ultimate form only within the confines of an exclusive, committed, secure relationship called marriage - it is only for our spouse.

For marriage to be what God intended it to be, more than mere sexual attraction and expression is required. It demands *eros* between two people who also *phileo* each other and are committed to one another in *agăpe*. As we mentioned in chapter 1, many marriages break down because sex is practised without the foundation and nurture of friendship and commitment expressed in transparent communication.

What does this have to do with planning and goal-setting, the subject of this chapter? Simply this: The creation of this foundation for marriage is too important to leave to chance. It does not happen by accident. Someone has to care enough to make it happen.

Our lives are characterized by stress and busyness to a point that leaves most married people exhausted. This applies to Christians as much as anyone. The result is that when we meet at home, we are too tired or tense to talk or listen much, if at all. We take refuge for relaxation in sleep or TV, and even sex is neglected because of exhaustion, differing interests or differing biological clocks. We are simply unavailable to each other.

I am reminded of a cartoon that expressed this problem of unavailability in unmistakable terms. The wife is facing a pile of dishes in the kitchen. The husband is seated in an easy chair, a crate of beer at his side. As he leans forward to switch on the television set, he says over his shoulder: *"Martha, is there anything you want to say to me before the football season starts?"*

Love, in the full three-legged sense of the word, does not happen by accident but on purpose. We need to plan for it and manage our time and energy to facilitate it. How do we do this? All the exercises that follow can and should be done individually, as a couple and as a family. Set aside time for planning and goal-setting, it will provide some of the most creative communication you have ever enjoyed.

PLANNING

We all need dreams or "visions" of things we wish we could do, become or have. Some of them may seem frivolous, and no doubt they are, but among them are the desires that motivate us. Psalm 37:4 says: "Delight yourself also in the Lord, And he shall give you (i.e. cause) the desires of your heart." If we have surrendered our lives to Christ as Lord, God has initiated a process of motivation by desire. God gives us a foretaste of what we can achieve, become or have through dreams and visions. He directs us into areas of ministry or responsibility, and stirs up a creative discontent that makes us long for and work towards his purpose for our lives.

We need to evaluate our desires against the standard of the Word of God. Although the standards of measurement may be different, we must realise that Christians are motivated in the same way as everyone else. The difference between Christians and non-Christians is not the presence or absence of goal-setting and planning, but the criteria or values we apply to the process. We differ not in the *mechanics*, but in the *dynamics*, of a well-managed, successful life.

DREAMS AND PRIORITIES

Begin, then, with a dreams list. On a clean page, record every dream and desire, everything you have ever wanted to do, become or have. Do not judge these dreams at this stage -write them down whether they seem realistic or ridiculous. They might become specific goals at a later stage. The function of this process is to get the juices of imagination flowing and thus facilitate creative planning and goal-setting.

Next, decide on your priorities. Make a list of every facet of life, every relationship or sphere of activity you are engaged in right now. Add those you wish you could include if you had the time. Do this individually, as a couple and as a family. Then decide on the order of priority of these items in your value system.

I will never forget a phrase I learnt from my roommate at university. He received some money (a rare commodity among university students) and invited a few of us to help him spend it. I cautioned him to go slowly, reminding him that he could not be sure when more would arrive. He laughed as he replied: "Money comes, money goes, memories stay!" I have often been reminded of that phrase when deciding what to do with the children on an outing and it helps, for better or for worse, to decide on priorities at home.

My wife and I are keen, if rather amateurish, gardeners. I once planted some bulbs and was watering them. A day or two later I saw in the flowerbed the giant paw prints of my bull mastiff. I immediately turned to find him so that I could discipline him. We saw each other at the same moment. He ran towards me, tail wagging, barking and looking for a game with the hosepipe. My first thought was: "I'd rather have a dog than a garden." That is placing the two items in order of priority. I did also ask him gently, not to put his big feet in the flowerbed again!

We all have a built-in, unspoken and often unexamined set of priorities, but we cannot manage our life, family or business without a clear understanding of what these are. It may be helpful to discover your priorities in reverse order. Let us say you have ten items on your list. If I told you that you could have only nine, which one would you relinquish? That item would be your number ten priority. Continue to let go of one item at a time. The one you would hold onto longest is therefore your number one priority item.

The following is an example of such a list of priorities. It in no way implies what your order of priorities ought to be. There is no such thing as "ought" in this context. Your priorities are real and you need to find out what they are.

ITEM	PRIORITY
Wife	2
Children	3
Work	7
God	1
Church	4
Friends	5
Gym	8
Golf	10
Study	6
Animals	9

GOAL-SETTING

Now draw up a time analysis sheet. This is a timetable of your usual weekly activities, showing the number of hours you spend on each. Draw up a second timetable, showing how you would like to adjust it. In other words, describe your ideal week. How would you like to arrange your schedule so as to accommodate your priorities? Include everything, even the specific times that you watch television, eat and so on. Note that the amount of time spent on an activity, does not necessarily indicate its priority standing. This is determined by whether I would allow other things to intrude on the time allocated to that activity. The sample time analysis sheet below illustrates what I mean. Below that, is a blank timetable for your use.

SAMPLE TIME ANALYSIS SHEET

TIME	MONDAY	TUESDAY	WEDNESDAY	THURSDAY	FRIDAY	SATURDAY	SUNDAY
07h00	Breakfast and take kids to school						
08h00	← Telephone calls →					Chores	
09h00		Appointment	MANAGERS	Appointments			
10h00	Office Admin		↓		Admin Mtg	&	Church
11h00						Shopping	
12h00			APPOINTMENTS				
13h00		LUNCH →					
14h00		Finance Committee Meeting	Office	Office	School Lifts		
15h00							
16h00	Gym			Gym	Sales Mtg	Golf or watch school Sports	
17h00		Family time and Supper					
18h00							
19h00	Family Night	Church Meeting			Date with [illegible] (eat out)		Church
20h00							

YOUR WEEKLY PLANNER

TIME	MONDAY	TUESDAY	WEDNESDAY	THURSDAY	FRIDAY	SATURDAY	SUNDAY
07h00							
08h00							
09h00							
10h00							
11h00							
12h00							
13h00							
14h00							
15h00							
16h00							
17h00							
18h00							
19h00							
20h00							

Having identified the areas in which you want to change, write each at the top of a separate sheet of paper, or in your electronic device. How do you want this area of your life to change? Your desire about this now becomes a goal. State the goal clearly, in terms that are SMART (Specific, Measurable, Attainable, Realistic and Time-linked). "It would be nice if we could spend time together" is not a goal but a wish. To change this into a goal, you would say: "I will spend one hour with my family every evening after supper, starting this evening."

BALANCE

As you consider your goals, establish whether they cover all the areas of your life in a balanced way. Are you giving a satisfactory amount of time and energy to each area? Each of us has 6 to 8 areas or dimensions of life that need attention. These include physical, intellectual, social, family, spiritual, financial, cultural and professional. If life were a wheel with six spokes, each representing one of these areas, would your wheel be balanced?

Allocate a score from O to 5 for each of these six areas (0 means unsatisfactory, 5 perfect) on the Wheel of Life diagram below in response to the statement: "In this area of my life I am sufficiently goal-directed, and getting the results I want". Make a mark on the appropriate spoke. When you have marked all six, join the dots to see what shape your wheel is in.

THE WHEEL OF LIFE

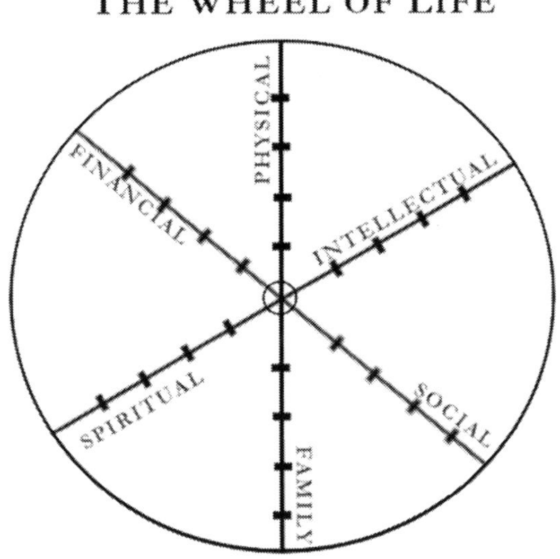

[31] Adapted from "The Wheel of Life" chart. Paul J. Meyer, Dynamics of Goal Setting (Waco: Success Motivation Institute, 1978).

How does your wheel shape up? Do you sometimes feel as though life limps along or that it shakes you up? I remember travelling to the mountains for a long weekend with 5 friends while I was at university. The car suddenly started to shudder and shake. The engine cut out, we stopped, started the car again, only to have it shake itself to a standstill once more. We made very slow, uncomfortable progress to the next town and took the car to the garage. The mechanic checked everything thoroughly, but couldn't find anything wrong with the engine. Later, someone thought of checking the wheel balance. A little lead weight had fallen off one of the rear wheels. I was amazed at the havoc an unbalanced wheel could cause to a motorcar!

I believe the same is true of our lives. The stress and busyness of modem life are much easier to handle when our lives are balanced. When they are not, the best engine in the world, fed with the highest octane fuel, will not compensate, and you could very well find that the faster you go, the more you shake yourself apart.

MOTIVATION

Having set goals and made sure that our lives are balanced, we need to ask ourselves: Why do I want to achieve this goal? What are the benefits that will accrue to me when I achieve it? Many people say that they do not do certain things because they lack the willpower. I do not believe that there is such a thing. What happens is that as we face the tasks we have set ourselves, we prepare a mental balance sheet of effort versus reward. Think of this scenario:

If l offered you 10 cents to run around the block, would you go? Never! But if I changed the amount to Rl0000, you would be running before I finished the sentence. The same amount of effort was demanded, but the greater reward made the motivational difference.

List every benefit you can think of that will result from you achieving your goals. The benefits should include internal ones as well as external ones, personal as well as what other people will think, big and small. Read the list every day, and especially when motivation starts to wane.

In our family we have a goals night when we do the exercises I have suggested together. We sometimes get a member of the family to tell us about the benefits she will gain on reaching a goal. We all play along to help her make the goal as exciting as possible. Playing the game of, "Wouldn't it be nice... " and "What would you feel when you reach this goal?" helps you to enjoy the benefits before they come to pass, and this supports your motivation and your faith in the realization of the goal.

If you are a Christian, I do not mean to suggest that we can or should engage in these exercises independent of God's purposes for our life. But we have management of our lives, under His guidance as the Chairman of the Board, and the sense of direction he gives us needs to be managed into the achievement of appropriate goals. The person who seeks to be the master of his own destiny is pursuing executive burnout of the highest order. But the one who leaves it all to fate and time, will find that not even faith can make the stagnant pond of their life less smelly!

PLANNED ROMANCE

By doing these exercises together as a married couple, you develop a habit of positive, creative communication. As you talk about "my goals, your goals and our goals", you are sharing your dreams and vision, and of course especially those that pertain to you as a couple. This is how you grow into deep-spirited friendship, a missing ingredient in many marriages. Make sure you marry your best friend- and stay friends by doing friend stuff daily, weekly, as much as you can.

Because the "Hollywood Syndrome" has taught us that you fall in love, get involved sexually, marry, and live happily ever after on this sexual energy, many couples never really become friends. When the romance wears thin, you may despair about your marriage. As you're reading this, perhaps all you have left is your commitment to each other. That is a good place to start. Build or rebuild your friendship through the goalsetting process. As you plan creatively for time together and adequate communication, you will discover a new intimacy and a natural growth of romance that will surprise and delight you.

You may want to plan your romantic times together. I read of a couple who tum their kitchen into a restaurant once every few weeks, and act as chef and waitress for their chidren, serving them exotically presented hamburgers. The children are put to bed early, with clear instructions to stay there. The couple then retire to their bedroom where a table for two awaits them with candles and a pre-prepared dinner. Romance doesn't have to be expensive!

Of course, the area of planned romance provides endless opportunities for either of you to surprise the other. Arrange for someone to babysit the children for the night, pick your partner up at work with a change of clothes and a toothbrush, and whisk her off to a show and a night in a local hotel. There are many ways to delight your lover.

But none of these romantic, renewing interludes will materialize unless someone plans them. Our tiredness is not an excuse for failing to set goals for intimacy, but is rather a further motivation to do so. Tiredness is usually the result of stress, and the single most common cause of stress is the feeling that I am not in control. What can change that? Goal-setting and self-management.

Our problem is that we are in a rut, and a rut is a grave with the ends knocked out! Get out of the rut before someone boards up the ends and fills it. And get your marriage out of the rut before the same thing happens to it. God did not design you for mediocrity or failure. As you get into step with Him, take responsibility for your life and plan, you will find an enjoyment of life you did not think possible.

Chapter Six

A PEDESTAL FOR EROS

Lovemaking does not begin at 10.30 p.m. when you are under the covers with the light turned off. Rather, being a good lover involves a lifestyle of romance, a skill set of creativity, an attitude of consideration and an environment of safety. The cartoon I described in the last chapter illustrates unavailability, but it is also a classic example of the boorish self-centredness that will destroy all feelings of romance, in even the most unselfish woman. I am reminded of one of these chauvinistic men asking his wife: "Why did God make you so beautiful and so stupid?" To which she replied: "He made me beautiful so that you would love me, and stupid so that I could love you!"

Romantic love or *eros* does not exist in isolation from the rest of our marriage relationship. It has to be nurtured and celebrated. The art of romance is the art of building a pedestal for eros. Let us look at some practical ways in which we can do this.

CLIMATE CREATION

Johnny was walking home from school looking sad when his friend Bill saw him. "What's wrong, Johnny?" asked Bill.

"Our house burnt down yesterday."

"That's terrible! Why don't you come home with me and your parents can fetch you later?"

When they got to Bill's house, he spoke to his mother. "Mom, I've brought Johnny for lunch - he hasn't got a home."

"No," said Johnny, "that's wrong. We have a home- we just haven't got a house to put it in!"

That mysterious something called a home is, in fact, an environment or climate. Just as each species of plant need the right position and environment climate if they are to flourish, so do people need a particular climate for their happiness and growth.

Pay attention to your home environment, and what it communicates at the point you are trying to initiate romance. Apart from obvious aspects such as tidiness, attention to the aesthetics of décor (flowers, fragrances, etc.) and tranquil, relaxing space and time, music, and most of all *availability* to one another without interruption (lose the cell phone!) make a statement of the value you place on one another, and of the sanctity of romance.

I am very aware that romance can blossom in unlikely settings, because it is primarily an attitude or predisposition towards each other. I was Lorraine's hopeful suitor for some months before our relationship became serious. I visited her one autumn morning, bearing nothing more romantic than a grapefruit which I cut and served to her on the balcony of her apartment. She tells everyone, to this day, that the flame of love was lit in her heart as we sat together after that prosaic breakfast on the floor, cleaning her numerous pairs of shoes!

The little extras like flowers also fall under the heading of the context for romance. Don't buy flowers only on special occasions or as a peace offering for coming home late - bring them as a gift, because they're her favourite colour, or because you both enjoy having flowers in the bedroom.

We need good powers of delegation and organization to create time together. Strict rules for ourselves and the children concerning "couple time" as against "children time" or "busy time" are important. Time for one another must be guarded jealously and not allowed to become cluttered with attention to the children's progress at school or unpaid bills. This is the opportunity to focus on one another and talk to each other, sharing our feelings and building up our partner.

Then there is the matter of confining things to their right place. The lounge where the two of you can relax at the end of a day, should not contain the tools from the weekend's repair work. The bedroom where you enjoy a few moments of intimacy together as you change out of work clothes into home clothes, should not be cluttered with the week's ironing or the children's school books.

Courtesy and consideration extend to both partners seeking to cultivate an environment in which romance can flourish. When the house is too much like a madhouse, a walk in the garden or sundowners on the patio may be called for. The point is that climate creation affords you a lifetime of opportunities to be creative. If your time together is boring, only you made it that way and only you can change it.

COMMUNICATION

If the goal of marriage is oneness or intimacy, and if intimacy is the totality of knowing, it follows that intimacy is not cultivated only in the isolation of the bedroom, and certainly not in an environment of self-centred lack of caring or interest in one another. Rather, intimacy should pervade every waking moment: from when you wake up and say "good morning", to when you touch in the passage on the way to the bathroom, from preparing breakfast together to a goodbye kiss; from a phone call for no reason other than to hear her voice, to when you pick up the children, go shopping together and spend time talking and dreaming, setting goals and communicating about yourselves to one another.

Many of the women I have counselled have raised, as the presenting problem in their marriage, the fact that the only time their husbands touch them is when they want sex. Romantic love expressed through touch, eye contact, flirting and other forms of acknowledgement of the presence and value of your partner, is a vital aspect of "climate creation".

Intimacy is furthered when you are involved together with the children and their needs, playing and praying with them and then tucking them in together. When you prepare supper and clear up together, sit together with your coffee or give her a foot massage and talk about your day, intimacy continues to build. Touch, smile, eye contact, care and embrace, culminate in the joyful self-giving and pleasure of sexual union.

Any number of enemies of intimacy seek to invade and destroy your union throughout this kind of day. They all fall into the single category of selfishness. The day I described is the ideal; for most of us reality is not conducive to such a totality of knowing and sharing. Requirements of work, family and community duties interrupt the best-intentioned romantic on most days of the week. You need to set aside time, prioritise time, and be committed to time to focus on one another.

It is, of course, normal to have individual interests and activities. All couples will be living life with an interplay between "His, Hers and Theirs" when it comes to interests, goals, time and attention. Intimacy does not mean doing everything together. You may have differing tastes regarding the use leisure time while you're in the same space. You have diverse talents and abilities, needs and availabilities. Selfishness, on the other hand, is an exclusive consideration of myself only in deciding on the expenditure of my discretionary time, energy and money. When I married I gave up the right to such exclusivity. This does not mean that I have no right to spend time, energy or money on myself - It means that such a right is exercised in the context of mutual agreement. "Self time" must constantly be balanced against "couple time", and joint responsibilities are to be borne jointly.

Some Christian authors and influencers believe that for men to be involved in child care and "housekeeping" is to lose their masculinity. Apart from this viewpoint reflecting very poor Biblical scholarship, I think a "masculinity" so easily lost is not worth defending! Far from losing anything, what is gained by sharing life, in the form of mutual interests, responsibilities, dreams and goals, is the very stuff of which unity and intimacy are made. When we marry we begin an adventure of making not just a house to live in but a loving environment, the making of happy memories together, and all those things that make a house a home. Which leads us to the consideration of climate.

COURTESY

Courtesy means simply the exercise of good manners. I said in chapter 4 that our marriage partner should be our best friend. Yet many marriages are so sadly lacking in the courtesies that we would extend to our friends, naturally, easily and without having to think about it. A greeting, a smile, making and maintaining eye contact, saying "please" and "thank you", are the least we would expect from a friend. In many churches it has become the norm to hug our fellow believers every time we see them. Yet we struggle to do this spontaneously for our spouses. We need to decide that we will (just for today), show our marriage partner the same courtesy we would expect to give to and receive from other friends. Make that decision every morning for a week - I dare you! I will say more about some of the specifics of courtesy later in the chapter.

CONSIDERATION

Consideration extends the concept of courtesy a little further. While courtesy gives others what I expect for myself, consideration seeks to give them what they need. It helps me to put myself into the other person's shoes. This presupposes that I have made the effort to understand her uniqueness.[32]

Consideration includes basic things like personal hygiene. To pay no regard to personal cleanliness and then to expect my partner to desire me sexually, is either inconsiderate or foolish. Women may be more sensitive to this than men, but there is a mutual need for understanding and consideration in this area. I have known marriages to fail because of one partner's refusal to brush his teeth!

A further aspect of consideration is physical appearance. To consider my partner means that I will want to look my best for her. It never ceases to amaze me that people who are meticulous about their appearance during courtship, when they know that gaining and maintaining the romantic favour of their intended depends on what they look like, can become so careless about this once they are married. Why is this? Surely their partner's taste or the chemistry of sexual attraction has not changed? Both partners need to pay attention to physical appearance, grooming and dress - usually men need more reminding to do so! But women need to remember that one of the established differences in the way we function sexually, is that men are aroused by what they see to a far greater extent than women are. Wives who show consideration for their husbands will want to do so in this important area too.

We knew a woman who would tell her husband as he went off to work: "Go and work up an appetite - but eat at home!" What a silly statement! Why, when his day at the office is a menu with colour photographs, advertising scrumptious cuisine of every kind, should he be enthusiastic about warmed-up leftovers when he gets home?

I heard that the reason why men gain weight once they are married is that bachelors come home, look in the fridge, find nothing

[32] An excellent source for understanding some of these aspects of uniqueness is a book, based on scientific research, by Willard F Harley, called His Needs, Her Needs - Building an Affair-Proof Marriage (Fleming H. Revell Company 1986 ISBN 0800717880

appetizing and go to bed. Married men come home, look in the bedroom, find nothing appetizing, and go to the fridge! A silly joke, but carrying an important reminder!

There are perfumes I buy for Lorraine that she puts on at the end of the day to enhance her natural attractiveness. Not only is the fragrance my favourite, but the fact that she puts it on for me makes coming home very special. The considerate spouse will celebrate their physical love for their partner by paying attention to their appearance and attractiveness, as much as they did in preparing for their first date.

NATURAL GIFTING

We have spoken about the joint activities and attitudes that foster an environment of romance. But what role does the natural gifting of each partner play in this process?

MASCULINITY

Peter advises men to *" ... live with your wives with the proper understanding that they are more delicate than you. Treat them with respect, because they also will receive, together with you, God's gift of life. Do this so that nothing will interfere with your prayers.". (1 Peter 3:7).*

What does he mean? Peter refers to the fact that women are "*more delicate*". Shock and horror, sound the non-PC alarm bells! In using this phrase, the Bible is first focusing on the obvious, which is that, in purely physical strength terms, women are, generally, not as strong as men. The reason why women don't participate in the same teams even if they play the same sport as men, is that they lack the same physical strength and hardness produced by Testosterone. This does not mean they are "weaker" in every sense! Women are, for example, renowned for their higher pain thresholds (we would probably have gone extinct by now if men had been the child bearing department!). However, Peter is, in this text, referring to how husbands need to consider (be aware of) how his wife is 'wired', and seek to complement her, and treat her as "different but equal". He is also instructing us in the oldfashioned value of chivalry. In my opinion, the exercise of a man's physical strength to protect, defend and care for his female partner, is not a Victorian idiosyncrasy that should vanish in the pursuit of sexual equality. I believe God has built this physical difference into the very essence of our nature, and in this respect he holds us accountable for our exercise of chivalry. It certainly also puts the matter of abuse of women by men in perspective. Very simply put, ANY man who abuses ANY woman, most especially his wife, and calls himself a follower of Jesus, blasphemes that Name, and disqualifies himself from the Kingdom of God. This is borne out by Peter's conclusion: " ...so that your prayers may not be hindered" The Greek word used means to "cut down, chop off or cut out". If the New Testament is right, there are many prayers bouncing off a lot of ceilings, in millions of well-intentioned but deluded men's homes, purely because those men are inconsiderate, insensitive bullies!

Men therefore play their part in climate creation when they take weight off their wives' shoulders, take responsibility for the care, provision and support of their families, take their share of housework, and do the "heavy lifting" work -without having to be nagged. Chivalry also includes noticing and complimenting your partner's physical beauty, grooming and dress. It is shown in pulling out your wife's chair at the dining room table or restaurant, or opening and closing the door of the car for her. A friend of mine advises young women in his church as follows. "When you go on a date, wait for the young man to open the car door for you. However, if you see him seated and eating his meal in the restaurant already, open the car door yourself and go inside!"

Lorraine had been an independent career woman for some years when I met her. I had to coach her in letting me be a gentleman in the ways I have described. It took some time, and she still forgets sometimes, but there is no evidence that it demeans her as a woman to be treated in this manner. Rather, I believe it celebrates her femininity, it shows her that I respect and honour her, I prefer her (and I also do it because she bashes the car door against the garage wall if I don't do it! (JUST KIDDING!)).

I do believe, however, that as marriage and life partners (what Peter calls "equal partners in God's gift of true life"), when a man expresses his masculinity in these ways he frees himself to be vulnerable, and his wife is similarly freed to express her femininity.

FEMININITY

What is the unique contribution a woman makes to climate creation? Peter again offers advice, instructing women to focus on the " ... *hidden person of the heart, with the incorruptible ornament of a gentle and quiet spirit ... " (1 Peter 3:4).*

Does this imply, even in the very patriarchal society in which Peter is speaking, that women's purpose is purely decorative? I don't believe that's what the New Testament implies at all. The portrait of the ideal wife in Proverbs 31 suggests the opposite:

> *Who can find a virtuous and capable wife? She is more precious than rubies.*
> *Her husband can trust her, and she will greatly enrich his life.*
> *She brings him good, not harm, all the days of her life.*
> *She finds wool and flax and busily spins it.*
> *She is like a merchant's ship, bringing her food from afar.*
> *She gets up before dawn to prepare breakfast for her household and plan the day's work for her servant girls.*
> *She goes to inspect a field and buys it; with her earnings she plants a vineyard.*
> *She is energetic and strong, a hard worker.*
> *She makes sure her dealings are profitable; her lamp burns late into the night.*
> *Her hands are busy spinning thread, her fingers twisting fiber.*

> *She extends a helping hand to the poor and opens her arms to the needy.*
> *She has no fear of winter for her household, for everyone has warm clothes.*
> *She makes her own bedspreads. She dresses in fine linen and purple gowns.*
> *Her husband is well known at the city gates, where he sits with the other civic leaders.*
> *She makes belted linen garments and sashes to sell to the merchants.*
> *She is clothed with strength and dignity, and she laughs without fear of the future.*
> *When she speaks, her words are wise, and she gives instructions with kindness.*
> *She carefully watches everything in her household and suffers nothing from laziness.*
> *Her children stand and bless her. Her husband praises her:*
> *"There are many virtuous and capable women in the world, but you surpass them all!"*

I believe that Peter's, and in general, the New Testament's view of femininity, speaks rather of the psychological style a woman brings to every pursuit, be it in the bedroom or the boardroom. Women in Bible times were primarily home-makers, yet that meant a lot more than it appears, as the Proverbs passage indicates. Women would create a home-based business operation, managing the employees, sourcing the products, co-ordinating manufacture and taking care of distribution, profitability and social responsibility. She was all of these things while at the same time creating an environment of harmony, love and "blessing" in her home, in the unique way only a woman can do.

The metamorphosis of many women into pseudo-men is one of the tragic by-products of the otherwise necessary goals of the feminist movement. The issue is not where women are active or what they do, but how they express themselves in their chosen fields. Emotional Intelligence, wholeness and feminine composure and self-assurance are a woman's most powerful and attractive assets in life and marriage. Peter highlights this as a spiritual responsibility, when he concludes verse 4: "*... which is very precious in the sight of God.*"

A woman is usually more predisposed than a man to pay attention to detail in the creation of a home. Decor and the things that are aesthetically pleasing, such as flowers and plants, table settings, curtains and furnishings, contribute to the creation of a place that provides a sense of physical, emotional and psychological wellbeing. It is not that men cannot do these things-(although many men need a lot of training to be able to!) - women just do them more naturally.

The traditional concept of a woman's touch in a home, and the fact that it is glaring in its absence, for instance in a bachelor's home, is perhaps evidence of a socialized predisposition in men. Men generally lack wholeness in their natures in this regard. The role of the partner who has the greater wholeness at any point, is to provide it and thus encourage growth to wholeness in the other party. Until my colour blindness is healed, I will remain unwhole to some extent, but I can and should be involved in talking about decor, helping to provide it and commenting on it in positive ways.

I love the beautiful surroundings my wife is so skilled at creating, and I am getting better at making helpful suggestions. In this respect I am like the preacher from the American South who said: "Ah know ah ain't what I oughta be, and ah ain't what I'm gonna be, but praise God, ah ain't what ah used ta be!"

On a lighter, but nonetheless very educational note:

WOMEN

Women are honest, loyal, and forgiving. They are smart, knowing that knowledge is power. But they still know how to use their softer side to make a point. Women want to be the best for their family, their friends, and themselves. Their hearts break when a friend dies. They have sorrow at the loss of a family member, yet they are strong when they think there is no strength left. A woman can make a romantic evening unforgettable. Women come in all sizes, in all colors and shapes. They live in homes, apartments and cabins. They drive, fly, walk, run or e-mail you to show how much they care about you. The heart of a woman is what makes the world spin! Women do more than just give birth. They bring joy and hope. They give compassion and ideals. They give moral support to their family and friends. And all they want back is a hug, a smile and for you to do the same to people you come in contact with.

MEN

Men are good at lifting heavy stuff and killing spiders.[33]

SPECIAL OCCASIONS

While we have been emphasizing the everyday aspects of climate creation, it is also important to emphasize special occasions, and our mutual role in catering for them creatively. Some people are raised to feel strongly about birthdays, while for others a birthday is just like any other day.

Loving attention to the celebration of a special day in the life of your partner or in your relationship, is an important feature of climate creation. I am sure we all remember days of celebration we enjoyed as children. We felt special and valuable because people lavished attention and affection on us. They sang to us, gave us gifts, cooked our favourite meals, took us on special outings, surrounded us with love and made us feel deeply cared for. That little wide-eyed child still lives inside all of us.

We said in chapter 2 that self-esteem cannot be stored up. It needs to be replenished constantly. We also said that you are the mirror that reflects your spouse's value to her or him. When you make an

[33] Author unknown. Quoted in Island Times, Palau (https://islandtimes.org/women-and-men/ November, 2017)

extra effort to make her feel special, you are investing in intimacy. You are providing the secure platform from which your partner can launch herself into the risky business of self-giving and love. Indulge the child in one another-with music, gifts, favourite food and special outings, even balloons and candles on the cake! Help one another rediscover the wonder of being special. It is in your power to make your partner feel loved- and you do not have to wait for a birthday or an anniversary. Why not do something out of the ordinary for no reason other than that she is special to you?

GIVING

We are all conscious of the caricature of the chauvinistic husband, who never remembers his wife's birthday or their anniversary, let alone buys her a gift. Some people focus on the quality and cost of the gift they give as the most important aspect of the celebration of a special occasion.

While a gift is a statement of the worth and esteem in which we hold a person (I know a man who buys *himself* a gift on his wife's birthday- I wonder what kind of statement that makes!), far more important than what we give, is the thought that goes into choosing the gift. The loving consideration involved in the purchase or making of a gift gives it value. People often say about a gift they did not want or one that was given as an afterthought: *"Oh well, it's the thought, that counts!"* An afterthought or a token gift does not count because it usually represents a lack of thought and therefore devalues the person receiving it.

We must be careful not to judge one another too harshly in this regard. Before one of my birthdays, early in our marriage, Lorraine was being very secretive about various shopping expeditions. I was excited because she was spending time in a shopping mall that housed my favourite bookshop (that, in turn, housed my favourite things- books!). The big day arrived and she asked to be dropped off at the mall again. I waited for her, literally able to smell a new book as I anticipated her return with my gift. She got into the car and, with a broad grin, handed me a gift-wrapped parcel. My first thought was: "This is a bit small for a book!" She has often subsequently described the devastated expression on my face and my brave attempts to smile and say, "Thank you, darling!" as I unwrapped and received her carefully planned gift- a calculator! She had seen me struggle to add up the figures of the monthly budget and thought a calculator would be welcome. All her love and forethought had gone into the selection of the gift. We have often laughed about it. I have since received more books than I have had birthdays, and Lorraine now uses the calculator when she does the monthly budget!

RECIEVING

Probably as important as making an art of giving, is learning the art of receiving. I have found South Africans notoriously inept at receiving gifts or compliments. I suspect that this is another symptom of a generally low self-esteem. Believing as we do that we are not worth much, we encounter a contradiction of that belief when someone says "You are looking wonderful!" or "I really appreciate you" or "This gift is just to say that I love you and feel very fortunate to have you in my life".

We find it difficult to cope with the tension or dissonance that these conflicting messages generate in us. So, we say something like: "Oh, I think I could do with a new hairdo/ diet I face-lift!", "Are you fishing for a favour?" or "Actually, I don't know how you put up with me!". A dress that is complimented is always "this old rag?", and a gift is received with nothing more original than "you shouldn't have!".

These responses are the equivalent of not listening. Our disregard says that we do not care for or love the giver, because we are incapable of believing that he really means what he says, and that we are valuable to him.

Another of my favourite "Peanuts" comic strips shows a lovesick Linus telling Charlie Brown about his first encounter with the little, red-headed girl he has desperately wanted to meet. The moment finally arrives, and Linus describes it afterwards:

"I couldn't say a word ... I just stood there all embarrassed and confused. I got so self-conscious I didn't know what to do ... "

The final picture shows him demonstrating a right hook as he concludes: "So I hit her!"

If your words come out in these defensive, awkward ways, receive a gift of love without words. A hug, a handshake or a kiss will more than compensate. Words of appreciation can be simple. "Thank you for caring" is as eloquent as a sonnet and is certainly better than some of the replies we have mentioned!

What is most important in this crucial exercise of climate creation, is that we demonstrate the ability to consider one another. Many of us will be starting from zero in this exercise and would do well not to expect to score a perfect ten every time. We need the humility to ask for advice and feedback from our partner to find out what she likes or dislikes about the present situation and how we can change things to please her. Preparing a candlelight dinner with French cuisine and background music provided by a string orchestra, for a guy who hates French food, only listens to John Denver and falls asleep when the only light is candlelight, is an exercise in futility. Creativity is important, but it should include consideration of one another's needs and preferences.

This area of building a pedestal for eros provides the ideal opportunity for communication, communication, and more communication - the subject of the next chapter.

Don't let the fact that you have married the girl mean the end of romance. Remember that you committed, not just to one honeymoon, but to constant romance, intimacy or *eros.* It will require daily attention and action.

Chapter Seven

INTIMATE IS AS INTIMATE DOES

The final few minutes of sleep are filled with strange images. The radio alarm intrudes with the announcer reading the 6 a.m. news. You say "good morning" to your spouse and children. You talk about your respective plans for the day over a hurried breakfast. You drive to work, observing the road signs along the way. You listen to a podcast or talk radio. You deal with colleagues and clients all day.

At lunchtime you read the newspaper.

You drive home.

Greet the family.

Walk into a living room piled with laundry, toys, dirty lunch dishes and litter.

Watch television.

Touch your partner as you pass in the passage.

Phone a friend.

Play with the kids while your spouse prepares dinner.

Have supper with your family, each member too preoccupied to talk.

Go to bed without attending to personal hygiene.

Turn your back on your spouse, and close your eyes.

Each of these activities has one thing in common - each involves communication. Someone sends a message that is received and decoded by someone else. We engage in a continuous process of interaction with ourselves, our environment, society, and an ever-narrowing circle of people we see, hear and touch in different ways throughout our day.

To exist as a human is to communicate.

We are communicating whether we are conscious of it or not. Our words, actions and attitudes, the environment we create, our facial expressions and body language, all contribute to the message we send or receive. Even silence conveys a message that may be positive or negative – it can mean comfort, agreement or anger. Failure to communicate, is in fact communicating, and can in fact convey a lack of caring. Touch is also eloquent, and has been shown to be essential to our physical and emotional wellbeing.

Additionally, the same code or medium can communicate different things to different people. A disembodied voice over the radio is an acceptable way of receiving the morning news, but is generally not a sufficient to communicate love to your partner. An untidy room conveys very different messages to the teenager who lives in it- ("But mom, I like my room like this!") -and the mother who has to walk past it at the end of a day spent tidying the house. To him it says "I'm comfortable!" To her it says "I don't matter!"

We have said that the existence of real love presupposes the practice of effective communication. Inadequate or superficial communication, as we saw in the poem in chapter 2, builds a wall of apathy that is the opposite to love. The three kinds of love, agapeo, phileo and eros, are all sustained by communication.

If an alien spaceship landed on our planet and an adult ET emerged, what would he see, apart from a ruined environment and the breakdown of urban life? He would see life, activity, hustle and bustle, traffic, people speaking, signalling, shouting, hooting, ducking and diving. And having exhausted his patience talking to a parking meter or two, a dog, a cow and an aloe, he would, perhaps with some difficulty, realize that the leader of all this craziness called Earth is its human populace. The following diagram suggests a process of discovery that might follow for the young interplanetary explorer, if he had the patience.

Levels of Communication

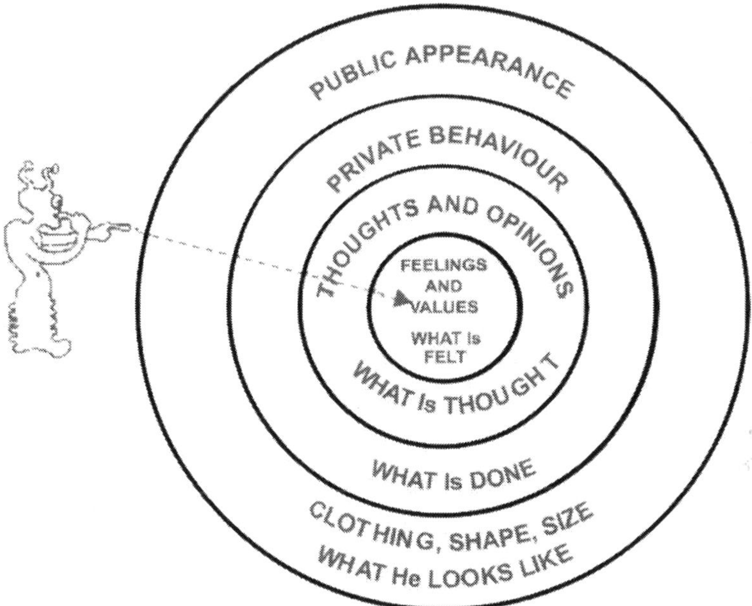

Beginning at the outer level of knowledge, as he spent time with groups, couples and individuals, he would progress to the centre of the target. But would he ever arrive there? And if he did, how long would it take him to do so? Furthermore, what kind of communication would be required for him to cross the boundaries of knowledge about human life? Where would he need to go to find this kind of communication? Would he see it in action if he came to your home?

COMMUNICATION LEVELS

John Powell has described five levels of communication[34] that suggest an ever-deepening level of "knowing" that occur in the communication process between two people. ET, or anyone wanting to understand human behaviour, would need to know what these are. As Powell described them, they are: 1. Talking in Clichés; 2. Reporting Facts; 3. Expressing beliefs and opinions; 4. Sharing Feelings; 5. Unedited Emoting ("Peak" Communication)

1. The cliché level, involves the social ritual with which we are all familiar:

   "Hello, how are you?" "I'm fine thank you. How are you?" "I'm fine too, thank you." This level is superficial and meaningless but necessary to what follows. No real self-disclosure is invited or offered. If you actually told the other person how you felt in reply to his question, he would be shocked, embarrassed or even angry with you for breaking the rules of the social "dance" you had begun.
   As a young adolescent I went to ballroom dancing lessons. The first classes were very intense and, in retrospect, extremely amusing. We were positioned at a particular point in the hall - the back left comer of the badminton court - to start a waltz. If, a number of bars into the dance, you made a mistake, you unceremoniously grabbed your partner's hand and headed back to the comer. You could not start the dance where you left off. There was only one way to begin. This is often the case with conversation. We should therefore not expect cliché level communication to do more than it is intended to.

2. The reporting facts level is exactly that. It involves sharing information about the weather, the children, people at work, the neighbours, the cricket score, and the stock market. It remains at a level that does not involve you. Your opinion is not asked

[34] John Powell Why am I afraid to tell you who I am?

or offered because it is unimportant to the moment. Most communication in marriage remains at this level. While it does, the marriage may seem very healthy but communication, and therefore intimacy, will in fact be superficial, because the individuals concerned are not offering themselves to one another. There is very little opportunity for "IN-TO-ME-SEE".

3. The beliefs and opinions level is the dangerous starting point of self-disclosure. We begin to say "I believe" or "I think", allowing the other to see the real me.

   In my work in the sales training field, I found that the single ***most important factor for success*** in sales was also the ***main reason why people left*** it, namely *believing in the product you are selling*. The power of such belief for success in sales is self-evident. If the salesperson doesn't really believe in what they are selling, they will not be successful for long. But, when I communicate my *beliefs* about something, I am sharing who I am. If you disagree with my beliefs, I will usually feel that you are rejecting *me*. Most people's self-concepts are too brittle to allow this. If l perceive the slightest glimmer of rejection while I am communicating a belief or an opinion, I will retreat to level 2. "I believe" will quickly become "They say that" or "I have heard that". Acceptance of me and my beliefs is, on the other hand, a "welcome" mat into the realm of self-disclosure.

4. At the disclosure of feelings level, I feel safe enough with someone to tell them how I feel about something. My sentences will begin with "I feel" and will continue with a word that describes the internal sensation associated with a particular emotion - tender, sad, happy, fearful, insecure, depressed. At this point I am running the risk of rejection that I would perceive as a devaluing of me as a person. Rejection can take many forms, be it ridicule, facial expressions of shock, embarrassment or cynicism, or, quite commonly, the other person trying to get me to explain or justify my feelings,

thereby taking me back to level 3. Examples of this kind of rejection will sound like: "Why on earth do you feel that?" or "That's crazy!" "Snap out of it!"

In our culture, men have often been socialized in such a way that they are unable to own, identify or explain their feelings. However, it is powerfully true that the only way to know that I am truly accepted is to take the risk of letting you see beneath my carefully constructed, rational exterior. This becomes possible as I have faith in you, commit myself to that faith, and reveal my commitment in self-disclosure.

5. The Peak level, as Powell called it, is the kind of communication that knows no fear of rejection. I therefore have no need to edit or even think about the way I communicate my feelings. I can share openly who I am and what I think and feel. I go beyond the level of talking *about* my feelings, to the expression of my emotions with freedom and transparency. Feeling sad or insecure is translated into tears, joy finds expression in helpless laughter, and the true tenderness of romantic love leads naturally to abandoned, intimate sexual expression. A caring, accepting person, who allows me to express my emotion without having to verbalize it perfectly, enables this healing level of communication to take place.

The sad reality is that 90% to 95% of all communication, including communication within most marriages, remains on levels 1 and 2. This does not mean that 90% to 95% of marriages never reach significant levels of real intimacy, but that only 5% to 10% of the time we spend together as married people has a chance of producing it. Level 3 is the crossover point between fact and thought-based communication on the one hand, and the sharing of emotional substance, while levels 4 and 5 are the only ones that truly have a chance of creating intimacy. If Intimacy is "In-to-me-see", it follows that we can only have real intimacy with someone with whom we share ourselves at an emotional level, and that such sharing automatically brings about intimacy between the sharers. This is often the reason people who have had extra-marital affairs give for their entanglement – that someone listened to, engaged with and mutually shared with them on a level of emotional transparency. I have had people of both genders telling me, or telling their spouse, that their extramarital affair was "not about the sex – it was that she really *listened* to me!" or, even more poignantly "when I spoke to him about my feelings, he looked into my eyes and invited me to tell him more!"

Does this help you understand why you feel so frustrated or why you or your spouse often feel that your marriage is providing less mutual understanding than it ought to? There is an inevitable correlation between input and output. It is therefore vital to pay attention to developing skills for effective communication. To love is to communicate - and communication is a skill that can and must be learnt.

COMMUNICATION MODELS

Models of communication are simply theories that help us to understand this process. The diagrammatic representation below shows us how communication takes place. It is my adaptation of the Shannon-Weaver Model.[35] S stands for the Sender, the person who initiates communication. M is the Message. R is the Receiver - the person with whom the Sender is communicating. C is the channel or Code used by the Sender and the Receiver. It appears twice because it represents both the *En*coding of the message by the sender and its *De*coding by the receiver.

It is important to understand that communication is a circular process. Sending a message in

the hope that someone will hear it is not communication. Even if a message is heard by the receiver, this is still not successful

[35] Shannon-Weaver

communication. Communication only takes place when a sender sends a message, encoded in a form that can be decoded effectively by the receiver, who hears it and responds to the sender with feedback to indicate that they have understood the message (or that they haven't understood it, and need more or adjusted information!).

In other words, the fact is that when you and I speak together, you will have only truly heard me when you are able to accurately restate the *content* and the *feeling* of what I have conveyed to you. This is the implementation of the "creative listening" we spoke of in chapter 3.

Let us consider in more detail each of the components in the communication process, with specific reference to the communication that takes place between marriage partners.

ADAPTED SHANNON-WEAVER MODEL

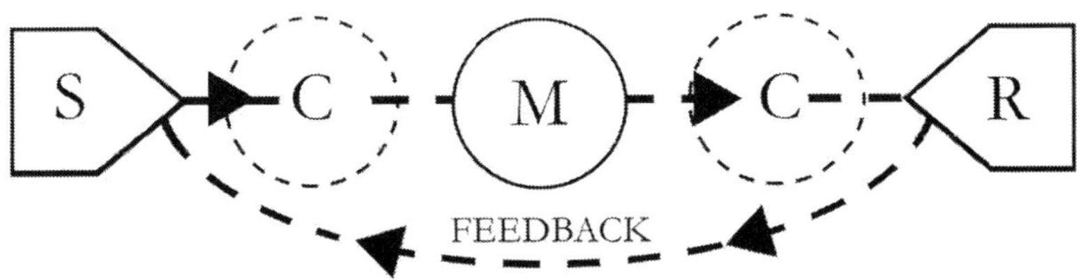

CODE

The factors that shape our view of the world are, to some extent, common to all people. Our senses, our memories, our basic emotions, our enjoyment of being touched, certain flavours, aromas, sights, etc., or the universal instinct of laughter, are examples of this. Other influences shaping our unique paradigms are derived from our cultural setting – things like the enjoyment of certain cuisine, musical and clothing styles, as well as aesthetics, etc. Others again are unique to each individual, and are an expression of personal taste in all the above-mentioned senses.

The mix of these three kinds of factors creates the code that an individual uses in their journey through life. They also influence communication – whether loud means angry or just enthusiasm; whether whispering is rude or polite; which words are insulting, inconsiderate, patronising or neutral, normal or acceptable. All of this has implications for the effectiveness of communication between two people.

Firstly, I must be aware that my code can cause puzzlement or a breakdown in communication. When someone does not understand what I am saying or is angered by it, it might be an invitation to re-examine my encoding of the information I am seeking to communicate.

During the end stages of World War II, the Allied high command, consisting of senior British, American and French officers, was meeting to plan a particular offensive. A small commission of four officers met to study the situation and present a report.

> After hearing the report, the Americans' response was, "This must be *tabled*." (The word "tabled" for Americans means "to be acted on immediately").
> The British reacted strongly to this. "No! It must not be tabled!" (For British people the word "tabled" means "to defer for a later decision" – and the British officers wanted it acted on immediately rather than deferred!).
> The two groups argued for some time ("It must be tabled!" vs. "No, it must NOT be tabled!", with the French looking on in puzzlement. Eventually a French officer had the presence of mind to ask, "What do you mean by 'tabled'?"
> When the code was supplied and the meaning of the word was understood, the two groups found that both wanted the same thing!

This kind of paralysis can and does happen in thousands of marriages in every society. We use codes in our communication that are not necessarily shared by our partner. When this happens, it is helpful and sensible to ask our partner what he means!

Secondly, I must recognize that words do not have the emotional content and impact for others that they have for me. This does not mean that my interpretation is better or worse than theirs – it is simply different!

One of the funniest moments in the Gilbert and Sullivan operetta "H.M.S. Pinafore", has the entire cast reacting with shocked disbelief when the Captain says "Damme!" (Damn me!). His outrage, and the reason for it, is completely overlooked in their reaction. The fact that he said the "d" word, becomes more important to them than any understanding of his reason for doing so:

"Did you hear him!
He said damme!
Oh the monster!
Overbearing!
Don't go near him!
He is swearing!"

The poor man is not heard or allowed to explain himself and is sent to his cabin in disgrace.

This often happens in our homes when we attach our personal intrinsic values, rather than the speaker's, to what is said. I remember feeling wronged quite early in our marriage when Lorraine described another man as "attractive". In my literalistic (il)logic, I thought that meant that she was attracted to him. I fell into a hole of despair, believing more and more as I re-played the tape in my fevered brain, that our brief marriage, my life and my ministry were over, that my life might as well end. A few agonising, sulky days later, I asked her what she meant when she said Jake was attractive. She explained that she thought he was handsome. I was extremely relieved to discover that she was not planning to leave town with him! Harmony and hope were restored!

Before judging what someone else means by what seems to be a loaded word, ask them what they mean by it!

Thirdly, I must have patience with my partner when my code is not received with instant understanding. I must allow time for the process of communication to take place, and resist the temptation to "shoot from the hip" when I am not understood. In most cases, the responsibility for accurate communication lies with the commincat*or*, or the sender. Poor communication has as much to do with poor *encoding* as with poor listening. Which brings us to:

THE SENDER

The sender initiates communication. Because he is a person with a unique mix of beliefs, feelings, experiences and values that have created his expectations and attitudes and world-view, the code he uses in every communication will also be unique. The following are several practical guidelines that will enable us to be more effective senders:

- **Avoid generalisation**. Sweeping statements are a sure way to block communication. For instance, what is your first reaction when your partner begins a sentence with "You always" or "You never"? You immediately go onto the defensive, and start to think of all the times you did not, or did, as the case may be. You are no longer open to hearing the problem or the feelings behind what your partner is saying. *What* is right is completely overshadowed by *who* is right. In the unlikely event that you cannot think up a defence, you react to generalisations with a sense of hopelessness. You feel that there is no use in trying to defend your situation. "You always", passes sentence on us: "You are hereby declared to be a habitual criminal, incapable of rehabilitation, of no use to man or beast." A generalisation is a character judgment. It offers no way out and therefore blocks further communication. It is therefore important to develop the ability to regard each occurrence of a certain form of behaviour as the first. Say: "I feel ... about that thing that happened today," rather than "You always ... ".

- Secondly, **use "I" messages**. The importance of this cannot be overstated. A sentence beginning with "I" is a clear signal of the desire for personal engagement with the person I am talking to. I am assuming responsibility for my thoughts and feelings. "They" messages, e.g. "*They* say", or "*People* think", are a disguised way of saying "I believe", or "I think" without taking responsibility, and thus without engaging. This takes the communication to a distant country where there is no possibility of self-disclosure. Similarly, a sentence starting with "we" is often a disguised form of attack or nagging: "*We* must take the rubbish to the dump". Think of this in your usual interactions, and keep it real!

- A final guideline for good communication is the use of self-disclosure as the goal of communication whenever this is appropriate. The more you care, the more of yourself you need to invest in an exchange with another. The other levels of communication are also important, and it is not always the right time, place or subject matter for self-disclosure, but we need to recognize that the usual problem is not too *much* but too *little* self-disclosure in marriage. Set a goal to engage in a minimum of 20 minutes of meaningful, self-disclosing conversation in every day. Begin where you are. Learn to convey your feelings with phrases like: "I feel like the way I felt when we had our first baby" or " ... the way I felt when I lost that job in 1978". This provides a good starting point for meaningful discussion. The skilful, caring listener will use it to draw out a greater measure of self-disclosure.

THE RECEIVER

The receiver, like the sender, is a person with a unique mix of beliefs, feelings, experiences and values that have created his expectations and attitudes and world-view. The code that a receiver uses to decode any communication will therefore differ from the code used by the sender. This is the simplest and most obvious reason why we get our wires crossed.

The receiver's responsibility is to listen. He must not only hear words and ascribe meanings to them, but engage in creative listening through a constant flow of feedback and affirmation, demonstrating a total involvement in the process of communication.

EFFECTIVE LISTENING

Listening has been called, "the greatest act of love any human being can show another". I believe this is a staggering indication of how scarce it really is. I often find people I am counselling, relieved and helped beyond description by the mere fact that someone has listened. I find this both humbling and infuriating. Why are people so conscious of the difference when a counsellor listens? Why is this so helpful? What would the results be if couples listened to their spouses effectively every day in their own homes?

Listening tells people that you care enough to want to understand them. If that does not create intimacy, nothing will. A man I counselled said: "Giving myself, my feelings and my pain to Anne, and listening to her has opened a door to communication in our marriage that has led to intimacy."

Listening is not just a matter of physically being marked present. It is possible for my spouse to be in the same room with me, even to look straight at me, and yet not to listen to me. The primary requirement for a good listener is physical, mental and emotional availability.

I often have people coming to me after a seminar session or a church service, wanting to engage me in deep discussion. In the past I tried to listen but found myself distracted, looking past the person at someone walking by, greeting a friend over his head, being reminded of someone I must talk to, and so on. My eyes would dart from the person in front of me, to others going by. I realized that the environment was not conducive to the kind of communication the person was seeking, because it affected my availability.

I have learnt to make an appointment with such people if our discussion requires more than a minute or two, or if it involves a complicated issue. Availability means that I sit (or stand) opposite the person, giving them full eye contact, relaxed and completely committed to them in terms of my time and energy. It means empathy, which comes from two Greek words, en for "into" and pathos for "feeling". To empathize literally means to "feel in", to put myself in someone else's shoes.

Secondly, as a listener, we need to be sensitive to the environment in which we are trying to communicate. If your spouse starts a conversation in an environment that is not conducive to your listening effectively, it is better to point this out lovingly, and agree to postpone the conversation or move to a more suitable environment. It is unfair to both of you to try to force the communication into a certain time and place.

On the other hand, our first pointer for listeners, availability, means that I may not simply keep deferring communication with "Not now, I'm busy" or hide in the workshop or the laundry from my spouse's need to talk. If now is not the time and this is not the place, love means that you will suggest an alternative: "Can we do this in about an hour? I'll meet you in the lounge for coffee and a chat."

ROADBLOCKS

There are two roadblocks to effective listening that we should be aware of.

The first is prejudice. Listening presupposes a nonjudgmental, unconditional acceptance of the person who is speaking. When we listen with prejudice, with implicit intimidation or rejection, we will hear selectively, if at all. We will be on the defensive: "I am only listening to think up an answer to what you are saying". I have tried to communicate with people who are prejudiced against pastors. Pastors, they suppose, are preachers, and preachers seek converts. Therefore this pastor is out to get me. One can see them buckling on their armour. I have felt as though I needed a can-opener to get within hearing distance.

Prejudice means to judge beforehand. That judgment can be one of several kinds. I can find the person guilty. This means that you assume that the speaker is wrong. He does not have the right to speak because his words are tainted.

Another kind of prejudice regards people as different and therefore inferior or superior. This view creates barriers of understanding and acceptance. It may show itself in people being shocked, angered or embarrassed by someone else's disclosure to them. Such a reaction cannot be hidden. It is seen in their facial expression or body language. The communication of such a response is bound to drive the speaker back to superficial levels of communication.

A second roadblock to effective listening is related to a physiological I psychological factor. We think at a rate of 600 words per minute, talk at about 120 words per minute and self-talk at approximately 1,300 words per minute.

What happens when you try to listen to someone? You go on a mental routemarch. You fill the large gaps in your attention by going off at tangents, following a chain of autosuggestion.

A couple I have been counselling have had some hilarious moments recently because of this phenomenon. He is a high-powered, very busy and usually preoccupied executive. One of the points of breakdown in their marriage has been this habit of taking mental routemarches.

His wife says, "I've been feeling fatigued- my doctor says it's low blood sugar." His self-talk runs something like this: Sugar ... When I was putting the sugar into my coffee at lunch today, I looked up and saw old Joe Cochrane coming into the restaurant. I need to speak to him about the contract he is fronting for me with the aluminium company. I really should have a dinner for the aluminium window manufacturers I'm doing the other contract for. Let's see - next Saturday is free. He replies, "You must have that seen to. Dear, would it be alright to have the Joneses from Wilkie's Windows around to dinner next Saturday?"

She feels unheard, neglected and injured. Counselling has taught him to "dial back" so as to listen to his wife with his full attention. In the beginning she could almost hear the cogs of his brain stop in mid-revolution and hear him telling himself to listen. He would look at her intently and ask her to tell him more about how she was feeling. She often caught him at one of these moments and giggled at the schoolboy concentration on his face. After a few months, listening has become a habit that he finds not only natural but enjoyable.

"I'm sorry I only learnt to do this after 14 years of marriage - I feel I've missed so much that Jill could have told me. Listening to her is fascinating!"

LOVE

Listening, like love, is a skill that can and must be learnt. A skilled listener is able to draw out the feelings of the person who is speaking. This calls for the kind of love described in the following acrostic:

L	Listening
O	Observing
V	Verifying
E	Empathizing

A letter in my file puts it this way:

Joe has learnt how to set aside his attacks and defences and to listen, then reflect, listen more and reflect again until I can say to him, "I feel you've heard me. You've not only heard my words but you've put yourself in my shoes, got into my skin and felt what it's like to be me.

MESSAGE

We have mentioned body language and facial expressions in talking about the message, the final component of the communication process we have been discussing. The message has its own independent existence. It consists of several things: the words used, the medium through which they are conveyed, the tone of voice, body language and actions of the sender (where applicable) and the environment in which the communication takes place. The words themselves obviously convey meanings. As we have said, those meanings can differ from person to person and from culture to culture. We therefore need to be aware of our encoding and decoding of them. The actual contribution of words to overall communication has been measured at a surprisingly low 7% of the total. If you think about significant exchanges with people, you will find that this is true. How many words of your spouse's marriage proposal or your acceptance of it do you remember? Even with more recent exchanges, you find that you remember and respond to an overall message and tone, often without being able to recall very many words. The medium is so significant that Marshall McCluhan, the well-known communications scientist, coined the phrase "the medium is the message". Think about your different reactions to receiving the following items of mail: an envelope addressed to "The

Householder", an airmail letter in a friend's handwriting, an account statement in a window envelope, an official letter from the Receiver of Revenue, a telegram. The medium conveys meaning.

The kind of care or interest a young man has in a young woman, is conveyed by whether he stops his car outside the house and hoots when he fetches her for a date or whether he comes to the door. The former will leave empty-handed if he comes to fetch one of my daughters!

The medium in interpersonal communication is usually a person, his voice, body language and behaviour. McCluhan's slogan therefore applies to all that follows. The tone of voice also conveys meaning to a significant degree. One can say the single word "yes" in four different tones of voice to mean: "Oh yes, yes, yes, of course, anything you want!", or "Yes, that is perfectly in order", or

"I'm not completely convinced, but for the time being I'll go along with it", or

"Well, it's no use arguing, so I'll comply, but don't expect joyful co-operation from me, sucker!" Because my tone of voice reveals my attitude, I need to consider my attitude ifl want my message to be accurately received. Tone of voice contributes about 38% of the meaning I convey. The remaining 55% of the message and its meaning is contributed by nonverbal means. These include body language, facial expressions and actions. Body language is regarded as an independent science. While much is written about it, the most important thing to realize is that body language conveys an overall message. The little isolated gestures are much less important than the big picture. Think about yourself. How do you present yourself to someone you are glad to see? How do you sit at a job interview? What happens to your posture when you feel intimidated or threatened? All people do not react identically in a particular culture, but there are common reactions.

We use our bodies to erect psychological barriers when we feel threatened. Turning sideways or crossing our legs or arms might signal, "Keep out". It may also mean that I have a sore left buttock and it is more comfortable to sit like that! If you are in doubt about what your paitner is telling you by his body language, ask. However, straight posture, close up, with full eye contact, certainly signals in my spouse an openness, honesty and desire to interact at every possible level. "No greater love has any man than this, that he lay down his newspaper for his spouse!" Facial expressions are also very eloquent in interpersonal communication. What do they say? Once again, they mean different things to different people. A man I know has a way of smiling when someone is speaking to him at a deep level. For years his wife believed he was mocking her or being sarcastic when he did this, and she withdrew from the exchange. I was with them once when she was speaking and he was smiling in this way. She stopped in mid-sentence and asked angrily, "Why are you grinning at me like that?"

He was hurt and confused. "I am trying to encourage you to go on. I thought smiling put people at their ease!"

He really meant the smile to be a sign of encouragement. Years of misunderstanding had resulted because his wife did not ask what it meant, and he did not realize that something was causing her to withdraw and become angry. I subsequently discovered that he does the same with employees and colleagues at work, and friends at the golf club.

We have probably all experienced what my father calls "tight skin disease", especially at about 2.30 p.m. on a Sunday, when we have had a large lunch and are sitting chatting to friends in the lounge. The symptoms are a full belly that exerts downward pressure on the skin at the front of the body, until it pulls the eyelids inexorably down into the "closed" position. This is often accompanied by a nodding and lolling of the head, lapses of concentration and occasional snoring. It conveys the message to the speaker that I am trying to listen, but I am just too tired.

How would you feel if you were the listener, as I was quite recently, and were really wide awake and alert, but the person speaking nodded off like this in mid-sentence? The message in all of this is simply that we must not make things too complicated. Facial expressions may send a message the listener does not intend to convey. We have all heard it said, and probably said our selves, that actions speak louder than words. Statistics bear this out. Actions contribute 33% of the 55% of nonverbal elements, that constitute a message and roughly 18% of the total message, as compared to the 7% contributed by our words.

Many men have to be taught the importance of saying "I love you" to their wives. Let us suppose that the husband concerned gets into the habit of saying this every day. What would happen to the wife's interpretation of his words if, having just heard them as he kisses her goodbye at the front door, she finds his clothes scattered around the bedroom, the bathroom floor covered with water, soapsuds, pyjamas, the basin displaying a ring of scum and beard stubble, the toothpaste squashed out along the vanity unit and the shampoo bottle lying on its side, capless, shampoo running down the wall? The warm glow of affection very rarely, if ever, survives a message of such uncaring slovenliness. We have mentioned the eloquence of touch. Positive actions like a hand on the shoulder, a hug or a hand cupping the face of a loved one, not only reinforce words of care and love, but amplify them at least 300 per cent.

A good communicator is one who will take pains to send a clear, integrated message. I am a whole person, and the message I communicate is conveyed through all the components we have discussed. Effective communication takes place, when the complementary contributions of these components are in harmony, rather than dissonance, and what I say is echoed by how I say it, my appearance, actions and the atmosphere in which I speak. When all these elements are in sync and I utilize these skills to engage in a process of disclosing my feelings, I am investing in intimacy. It is an investment that will never be eroded and will never fail to render handsome dividends.

This chapter forms the heart of this book, and is central to the advice I give couples in my counselling programme. It is not only my best advice, it is the lifeblood of real intimacy, the antidote to estrangement, and the key that unlocks the door of God's purposes for your marriage.

NOTES:

1. John S. J. Powell, Why Am I Afraid to Tell You Who I Am?(Allen: Tabor Publishing, 1969).

2. Merrill R. Abbey, Communication in Pulpit and Parish (Philadelphia: Westminster Press, 1976), pp. 28 - 30.

Chapter Eight

AND SO TO BED

Stop cheating - you are supposed to read the first seven chapters before you read this one! I know that most people turn to the sex part first to see how brave the author is on the subject. I also know that some bookstores refuse to stock books that are too explicit on the topic. I want to be as honest as possible within the context of the subject of intimacy, which is my major concern, but a full treatment of sexual issues is not possible in a volume as brief as this one. We will discuss sexual matters to the extent that they apply to what I have said thus far.

THE CONTEXT

The Bible speaks of sexual intercourse as "knowing" one another. This implies a spiritual, emotional, psychological and physical oneness. We have seen that the purpose of marriage is to create intimacy between two people. We have described intimacy as a totality of knowing, a process that takes place through self-disclosure. We said that communication is a skill that can be learnt. As that skill is applied to every area of our lives, a climate is created in which the natural expression of sexual love is encouraged. Sex is not a substitute for intimacy but the culmination of oneness. It is in sexual intercourse that the totality of knowing is given its fullest expression, provided that it is prepared for and accompanied by the sharing of thoughts, feelings, desires and commitment. Two people who are committed to one another, trust, talk to and enjoy each other, share one another's values and interests and pray together, have laid the foundation for real intimacy.

We have also said that the desire for oneness is built into every human being. We long for it and seek it, and are dissatisfied with anything less. Promiscuity fails to meet this need, and those who embrace an immoral lifestyle often tum to drugs or alcohol to anaesthetize the pain of loneliness. Research has shown that even prostitutes are aware of this deep need for closeness, they are careful not to express or feel emotional attachment or even physical pleasure during their professional activities. They may overcompensate for this in the contempt or disgust they feel for their clients.

As you apply the principles for the creation of intimacy and tenderness in your marriage, sexual expression will follow regularly, easily and spontaneously. Planning for intimacy as we have suggested, is not meant to rule out spontaneity and the need for unusual initiatives in sex. Sex has a built-in spontaneity because it is a response to the passionate affection you feel for your partner. That passion can overtake you while you are preparing a meal, walking in the garden, swimming at midday or painting a room. Either of you might take the sexual initiative at such a moment, provided that sufficient privacy can be arranged. Sex is meant to be fun.

The scriptures exhort a man to enjoy or rejoice in the wife of his youth, to be ever captivated and satisfied by her love (Proverbs 5: 18-19). The sexual revolution has released women from inhibitions with regard to taking the initiative in sex. I think this restores the biblical norm. Whereas flirtation and pursuing men for sexual reasons was certainly not the norm, biblical passages such as the Song of Solomon, bear repeated testimony to the young woman seeking out and initiating sexual love with her bridegroom (see, for example, Song3:l-4, 8:5)

As your sexual love leads you towards the consummation of your desires and you go to bed, take two things with you: the realization of God's joy and his approval of your sexual love for each other, and consideration and celebration of your partner, as a gift from God, to be received with joy and treated with care.

Eros is rooted in desire and is thus self-directed. Agapeo is a self-giving love and is other-directed. Both kinds of love are God-given. Each is necessary to balance the other and to order your sexual relationship.

GOD AND SEX

Sex is the creation of God and is given to the human race as a special blessing (Genesis 1 :28a). The difference between humans and animals in this regard is that for animals, sex is seasonal and purely physical. While some species of animals gain exclusive sexual loyalty through mating, their sexual expression is rarely, if ever, for anything but the seasonally induced, almost automatic purpose of breeding.

For humans, sex is an open season. It is not merely for reproduction, but is a way of expressing psychological and physical union and exclusive commitment. Some may think that this is a curse rather than a blessing, but accountability is an inherent part of the sexual relationship in marriage. God designed it to be holy and good. To use such a gift for self-centred, inconsiderate or destructive purposes, is to invite spiritual disillusionment and disaster. God's laws are not petty but purposeful. Obeying them brings wholeness to our lives. We do not break God's laws -ignoring or violating them breaks us. What are God's laws? A detailed reading of the Old and New Testament reveals that God outlaws only those sexual activities that have long been regarded as perversions. Included in this category are bestiality, incest, rape and sodomy or homosexuality. God expresses his revulsion for all of these and calls them abominations. Also forbidden, although not for the same reason, is intercourse between a man and his menstruating wife. This was probably for reasons ofhealth and because of the ceremonial significance ofblood.

As regards sex in general, the Bible says very little about the how but focuses on the who. We will discuss the "how" aspects later. Sex is seen as a holy act, to be engaged in between a husband and his wife for their mutual wellbeing and pleasure. Outside this mutual commitment, as in premarital or extramarital sex, prostitution or self-centred abuse even of a marriage partner, sex is offensive to God because it destroys the participants.

The church has had a very poor track record in presenting sex as holy and good. For centuries it taught that sex was for procreation only, and even then it was sinful to enjoy it. Theologians taught that the Holy Spirit left the room when a married couple made love and that abstinence was the higher virtue. Such attitudes were carried into postenlightenment societies, such as Great Britain, in the form of the numerous sexual taboos of Victorian society. Contemporary society has inherited much of this, as well as the even stricter controls of our Calvinistic European heritage, to produce a culture in which sex and God, or sex and good are mutually exclusive terms.

Most people born before 1960, and many born after that, never discussed sex openly with their parents, but learned about it from their friends at school, amidst ribald joking, so that it gained the connotation of being dirty. The stork is still a familiar alibi to explain where babies come from. Sexual organs and sex itself are talked about in innuendos.

These religious and societal taboos have a real impact on sexual attitudes within marriage, and affect the levels of activity and satisfaction through that activity, for both partners. I knew a couple who had married after each had lost his first partner. The wife had had a hysterectomy. The husband asked me to come around and counsel them.

"Our problem," he explained, "is that Betty is unable to have children".

"Go on," I replied.

"Well, we've been married for three months now and I'm getting frustrated. I can't handle it!" "Handle what?" I asked.

"The part about no sex," he replied.

He had been taught, and sincerely believed, that sex was only for procreation. What a relief that I could show him that sex was for other purposes too, and that they were free to enjoy it in their marriage. The need to unlearn false perceptions and get back to biblical truth about sex is self-evident.

In 1 Corinthians 7, for example, Paul predates the sexual revolution by about 1900 years when he says that sexual relations are for the mutual satisfaction of each partner by the other (verses 3-5). Research has shown that until the late 1950s, orgasm for married women was largely regarded as optional and even unnecessary, and experienced rarely and then only by happy accident. The sexual revolution of the 1960s changed that, but even so thinking has only recently caught up with what the Bible mooted as the norm centuries ago.

The negative effect of the sexual revolution has been an obsession with what we get from our newfound sexual freedom. We would do better to focus on mutual giving as the goal of sexual activity in marriage. So, for instance, the New Testament uses the words "deprive one another" (verse 5) to describe the consequence of abstaining from sex. Anything less is, in fact, a form of masturbation because it seeks self-stimulation and satisfaction and neglects togetherness and intimacy.

THE PURPOSE OF SEX

What are the functions of sex in marriage? Although there are several, I believe that they are all secondary to the central purpose of intimacy. Sex is intended to foster that totality of knowing we have discussed. This includes communication, giving and receiving pleasure, physical and psychological release, and the procreation of children. Let us consider each of these.

COMMUNICATION

Communication and sex go hand in hand. One of the taboos that is the most difficult to overcome is that sex should not to be talked about: sex is nasty and dirty and only bad people talk about it. An attitude like that negates an important area of intimacy for couples. Every married couple develops their own code for sexual matters. Perhaps he switches off the television and says, "What about an early night tonight, dear?" Perhaps she brings him coffee wearing a certain negligee. The old joke about women always saying "I have a headache" prompted another joke.

A husband walks into the lounge with coffee and an aspirin for his wife. "What's the aspirin for?" she asks.

"For your headache," he replies.

"But I haven't got a headache."

"Great! Let's go to bed."

Better than all the above is the simple approach of talking about sex with your partner. No hint, expectation or nagging will provide the arousal that comes from a simple sentence: "You are more exciting to me than ever - may I have a date with you in the main bedroom in about 20 minutes?" When the frequency of sex diminishes, talk about it. Evaluate your level of satisfaction on a regular basis. Talk about your expectations and compliment one another's skills, appearance and desirability.

Talk during sex too. Intercourse is not the time to play guessing games. Rather, have a rule that says loving, positive direction is welcome and desirable. Comment favourably when your partner does something right, and remind him to repeat the performance next time! Endearments and loving affirmation of your partner during intercourse will promote intimacy and provide increased satisfaction for both of you.

Some sex therapists encourage couples to conjure up in their minds an ideal sexual episode while making love with their partner. This does not apply only to fantasizing an ideal environment like a tropical island. They are taught that it is acceptable to picture themselves making love to someone else if their partner does not arouse them. This is not only an act of mental adultery but is as destructive to intimacy as actual sexual infidelity. The kind of frank communication we have discussed, with each partner talking to and about the other, focuses you on the person you are making love with as the object of your sexual love.

Of course, communication in the sexual context is not only verbal but nonverbal as well. A woman I counselled felt that she and her husband were losing intimacy in their sexual relationship when they no longer kissed during intercourse (see Song of Solomon 1 :2). Seek to maintain the total communication process that keeps you involved and fosters intimacy with your partner in these ways.

PLEASURE

The giving and receiving of pleasure is another purpose of sexual intercourse. We have already stressed the need for balance between self-giving and enjoyment to maintain the energy of sexual love. The verb translated "rejoice" in Proverbs 5: 18 has been rendered as "take pleasure" in another translation. Not only is pleasure in sex not sinful, it is part of its blessing. Passionate involvement in enjoying your partner sexually is the trigger to your ability to please her. Thoughtful, creative planning of your romantic life leading up to and including intercourse, is necessary to the communication of real love. Plan it so that it gives both of you pleasure. A clumsy fumble in the dark, with no forethought or care in the interests of a false morality, is a negation of taking pleasure in one another, and therefore dishonours God.

RELEASE

Sex functions, as a means of physical and psychological release for both partners. When sexual release is absent for long periods of time, we experience increased tension, loss of alertness and loss of self-esteem. The normal male has a semen build-up that reaches capacity every 48 to 72 hours. A friend of mine, on hearing this, commented, "Well, that's one way God designed to make sure men talk to their wives at least once every three days!"

A popular myth held that women's need for sex is much less than men's, and that orgasmic release is far less important for women than for men. There is no evidence to support either of these views, and they seem to contradict the biblical emphasis on mutuality in sexual giving. If a husband's body is for his wife's pleasure (1 Corinthians 7:4), and she is designed as an orgasmic being, what form should this pleasure take? Why should her needs be different to her husband's? I believe that such myths are part of the oppressive system of rationalization that surrounded Victorian patriarchal society, and that the only people still propagating them are men who are lazy and therefore lousy lovers.

Real love, and therefore the pursuit of true intimacy, involves the stimulation by each partner of the other to the point of the climactic release of orgasm. In fact, my contention is that the highest form of intimacy, and therefore the desired goal of sexual intercourse, is simultaneous orgasm. Some authors on sexual technique do not see simultaneous orgasm as necessary, and certainly failure to achieve it every time is not the end of the world. But I believe that two people who care enough for each other will, in the course of their marriage, learn how to pace themselves and one another sufficiently well to make this goal achievable most of the time.

I will say more about the techniques required for simultaneous orgasm when we consider the individual satisfaction curves later in the chapter. Suffice it to say that the totality of knowing what we have been talking about finds no higher expression than that found in simultaneous arrival at the climax of love making.

PROCREATION

The last purpose or function of sex I mentioned is procreation. I do not mean that it is to be sought as the result of every act of intercourse. We have the ability to produce life through sexual union. As Christians we see that as a gift, and therefore as an area of stewardship -as parents we are managing another's property. Our ability to produce children should therefore be seen as part of that stewardship. It is to be managed or controlled. One of the major hindrances to sexual satisfaction and self-giving is the fear of pregnancy. We eliminate this fear, and therefore free one another for self-giving, when we take precautions against unplanned pregnancy. We also demonstrate responsibility before God for our procreative power when we do so.

What is important in this context is, however, our attitude to pregnancy and methods of birth control. Although we use reliable contraceptives or take precautions, we must maintain an attitude of openness to the possibility of having children, in the event that these malfunction. One of my difficulties with the pro-abortion lobby is the fact that it is a symptom of the unwillingness of our generation to accept responsibility for our lives. When we decide to marry and engage in sexual activity, we are entering a realm where the consequence of our choices-in spite of wise stewardship and technology -is procreation. When we try to reverse this by abortion, we are not only committing murder but evading our responsibility as adults. To be an adult is to accept responsibility for our actions.

You are right to conclude that I am vehemently opposed to abortion. Although this is not, in the first place, a book on ethics, abortion falls under the broad heading of sexuality. As a counsellor, I have had to agonize too often with people suffering the devastating effects to their consciences and emotions of having had an abortion, to have anything good to say about it. Abortion is a gruesome infringement on the rights of the unborn child and is, by definition, murder.

Many people use certain methods of birth control, unaware that their function is in fact abortive. The backup function of intrauterine devices (the coil, the loop and the copper T), is to prevent implantation or to terminate pregnancy at an early stage, if they fail to prevent fertilization. Certain oral contraceptives, such as the synthetic progesterone pill, prevent implantation of the fertilized egg, by changing the mucus pattern of the uterine wall. The "morning-after" pill may function in a similar manner. In pursuing peace of mind by reducing the fear of pregnancy, Christian couples need to make their position clear to their physicians, and ask them to prescribe one of the many other methods of birth control that are not abortive in function.

ATTITUDES TO SEX

Eighty percent of the sexual dysfunction experienced in marriage is a result of a wrong attitude. Problems such as impotence and frigidity very rarely have physical causes. They are usually connected to attitudes such as performance anxiety, set ideas about sex or low self-esteem. We will deal with three categories of attitudes: those to our own and our partner's sexuality, to our bodies, and to the sex act.

SEXUALITY

Sexuality is a wonderful aspect of God's creative genius. It is woven into the shared humanity of a man and a woman, yet it is mysteriously different in each of them. What is shared draws them to each other while their differences force them to take the time and trouble to learn about each other, so that their coming together will not cause more pain than pleasure. Our attitude towards our sexuality should be one of celebration and joy and, at the same time, humility and awe. Our sexuality is mysterious and fascinating. As David says: " ... I am fearfully and wonderfully made ... "(Psalm 139: 14).

Some of the consequences of the sexual revolution, the explicit flaunting of sexuality in pornographic magazines, and the portrayal in movies of sex divorced from relationship and intimacy so that sexual performance has value in itself, amount to the destruction of our humanity. The same is true of many of the sex manuals on sale today. Sex technique alone will not satisfy our deep need for intimacy. Sex education in our schools or homes that does not teach our children how to develop intimacy in their sexual lives, contributes to the problem.

We need to realize that our sexuality is related to every other area of our life. Sexuality and its expression is inextricably linked to conflict, self-esteem and stress. To love our partner means to take these things into consideration. We need to resolve conflict before we go to bed. We must provide a place where our partner can air his frustrations and where, through loving consideration and listening, we can create a climate of intimacy. The same is true of the dynamics of self-esteem.

I remember a time when I faced the failure of a dream. A project that had been very important to me was crumbling. People had disappointed my trust in them. The work I had done seemed to have been in vain. There was financial privation for our family. I had never felt so low. My confidence was shattered. I was trying to find work and experiencing the humiliation of going for interviews and being turned away. It was the first time in ten years of marriage Lorraine had seen me in this state.

I tried to seem confident and in control, so that I would not frighten her or cause her to lose all respect for me. We were talking one day when I suddenly felt as though I would explode ifl did not share my pain with her. As she listened, I exposed my insecurity and inner conflict. Her response was the opposite of what I had feared. Her strength and confidence boosted mine. Her affirmation of me began to restore my self-esteem. It was an experience that increased rather than reduced her respect for me, and the intimacy between us was never more beautiful than at that moment.

Stress affects us physiologically. It reduces the ability of our blood vessels to dilate as they have to for sexual function to take place. Impotence in men and pain during intercourse for women can therefore be the result of stress. A more obvious physical cause of sexual dysfunction is fatigue which slows down the metabolism and therefore the hormonal function necessary for sexual intercourse. I have counselled young couples planning their weddings to consider postponing the sexual consummation of their marriage until the next morning rather than force their fatigued minds and bodies and make a bad start to their love life. Planning the wedding day so that it will not be too exhausting is an alternative-do not wait until midnight before leaving the reception.

A final matter of attitude as it applies to our sexuality, is to affirm and consider the sexual differences between men and women. A man's sexuality has very delicate connections to his mental processes. He is aroused mentally and can control himself mentally - a man who is battling with premature ejaculation could help himself by thinking about his bank balance as the critical moment approaches! What a man sees and pictures in his mind directly affects his sexual performance. He needs his wife to be his mistress too, to dress, care for herself and make herself up in a way that he finds attractive. The sexual :function of the man also needs physical stimulation. The sensitive, caring touch of his wife is also essential to his ability to function. His sexual satisfaction is dependent on the manner and duration of intercourse. We will discuss this in more detail later in the chapter.

The sexuality of women is both dissimilar and similar to that of men. A woman also needs certain mental stimuli to be able to :function properly. The emotional climate and the environment must be right for her sexual love to thrive. Her sexuality is dissimilar to the man's in that it is aroused by physical touch and stimulation. She is not ready for intercourse at the drop of a hat, but needs to be brought to that point by the loving touch of her husband. We will also consider some of these physical aspects later in the chapter.

Both men and women need to establish a good attitudinal base to their own unique sexuality and the functional uniqueness of their partner. A woman who does not understand her own sexuality, and has a husband who is ignorant and insensitive in this regard, and tries to give expression to his sexual drive more often than she thinks of doing, might develop the attitude that men are animals because all they want is sex. She may not have patience with her need to be brought to a point of desire by foreplay and, because she is not aroused, she may conclude that she does not need sex. A husband who expects his wife's eyes to light up at the mere suggestion of sex, may become impatient and angered by her attitude because he does not realize that she needs more stimulation before she will even want to function.

I know couples who joke about their vastly differing libidos, but I believe that merely accepting such tension in their sexual lives is an avoidance mechanism. The better way would be for them to acknowledge that they function differently, but that they both need sexual love. A wise, considerate, loving husband can, I believe, create in his wife a new responsiveness and joy in her sexuality. Many couples' sexual problems can be traced back to bad experiences on their wedding night. Insensitive young bridegrooms can make sex a fearful thing to contemplate in their wives for ever after. Correction of attitudes on both sides can undo the damage.

BODY IMAGE

The second major area for correction is our attitude to our bodies. As he contemplated the creation of his own body, King David said: "I am fearfully and wonderfully made". He celebrated his physical being. The Bible uses the phrase to "uncover the nakedness" of another to refer to sexual intercourse (see, for example, Leviticus 18: 15).

God's perfect people in Eden were "both naked ... and were not ashamed" (Genesis 2:25). The Bible commands a young husband to rejoice in the wife of his youth: "Let her breasts satisfy you at all times; And always be enraptured with her love ... " (Proverbs 5: 19). The Song of Solomon speaks explicitly about the physical and sexual attributes of the man and the woman that captivated each other. The biblical norm is an open acceptance of my body and of my partner's body.

I know people who take such an excessive view of modesty that they have never seen their spouse naked in the course of a lengthy marriage. Couples may differ, for instance, on the question of whether to have lights on or off during love-making. This may be related to the poor self image of one of the participants or it may merely be a matter of taste.

The correction of our attitude to our bodies may mean that we need to come to a new acceptance of our partner's body and a celebration of her beauty. It may mean caring for our body as a temple of the Holy Spirit through diet and exercise. We are to love ourselves, and develop a healthy self-image based on the fact that we are made in the image of God. We may also need to nurture a caring acceptance of our partner's gift to us of her own body. I do not own my wife's body, but because she gives it to me, I am a steward of it. I can do this by being empathetic with my wife about her fear of pregnancy, during the course of pregnancy and at the time of childbirth. I have known men who have a desire to have as many children as possible, for religious or selfish reasons. They inflict pregnancy upon pregnancy on their wives, without any thought of sharing the burden. Men who refuse to be present when their children are born, not only rob themselves of a miracle but display a lack of empathy that rightly earns them the scorn of women who are more noble than they are.

THE SEX ACT

The final area in which attitude correction may be necessary is our view of sex. I have mentioned that 80% of sexual dysfunction is caused by performance anxiety. The question that plagues many is whether we can satisfy our partner sexually. We have been conditioned by the sexual revolution. The media have told us about the qualifications for sexual prowess: the size of sexual organs- the size of a woman's breasts and whether they are "lifted and separated", and the size of male genitals. The fact that such criteria have nothing whatsoever to do with the ability to function or satisfy our partner sexually, must be underlined and allowed to change our attitudes towards sex.

Behind the attitude of performance anxiety lies the most destructive legacy of the sexual revolution, the idea that sex is merely an animal function. When sex is divorced from intimacy, even being good at it demeans us.

A healthy alternative is the understanding that sex is a fulfilment of my personhood or being. I do not need to perform a sexual function but simply t be who I am as a sexual person. Then the expression of totally involved sexual love is an end in itself which cannot and does not need to be graded on the curve. Sexual expression of true intimacy is always good sex.

Another attitude that inhibits sexual enjoyment is the belief that sex is dirty. It is evidenced by feelings of shame about sex, frigidity or impotence, the inability to talk about sex or the use of innuendos in doing so. We have said that sex is God's good gift to us, that it is holy and good and that pleasure in sex is not sinful. As we allow these truths to renew our minds and determine our attitudes, we will find joyful abandon and gratitude to God in our sexual expression.

Some people fear sex because they fear the loss of control that it implies. Passion and ecstasy are appropriate in the sexual context, and fear of these feelings is usually a symptom of a deeper fear. A woman who feels unsure about her husband's love and the strength of his leadership will be reluctant to abandon herself to him during lovemaking. The fear and its possible causes need to be addressed so that the sexual area can be corrected.

Competitiveness between marriage partners, together with some of the wrong attitudes to sex that we have discussed, may produce the poisonous view that sex is a weapon to be used to have my way, prove a point or reward good behaviour. Withholding sex as an act of spite, punishment, revenge or manipulation is incredibly destructive. Because sex is so close to our deepest identity, our partner's reactions to our sexual advances will have far-reaching effects on our self-esteem. Frigidity and impotence can result or a partner may turn to extra-marital sex to regain his self-esteem. No grievance or loss of dignity or worth justifies infidelity, although it might explain it. Remedying the situation would call for as much attention to the cause as to the effect of such unfaithfulness.

A final attitude for our consideration that leads to a discussion of sexual technique is the one that if we do what comes naturally in sex, everything will work out as it should. This attitude is most often displayed by men and is the cause of considerable frustration in many marriages. It is motivated by a sense of superiority or pride. Such men feel that admitting that they need help or direction in their sexual conduct would mean an irretrievable loss of their masculinity.

Let us consider, in purely physiological terms, what happens if this attitude rules a couple's sexual life. The graphs depict the respective patterns for men and women in terms of the relationship between the time taken in intercourse, and their progress to orgasm.

If a man simply does what comes naturally, he will reach his climax, lose energy and most likely fall asleep before his wife is fulfilled. Far from acting according to his instincts, a man needs to be considerate and to pace himself

NATURAL PROGRESS TO ORGASM

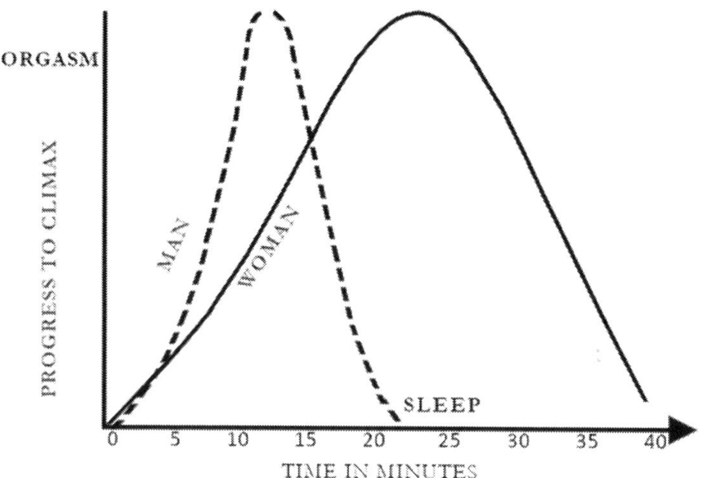

SIMULTANEOUS ORGASM

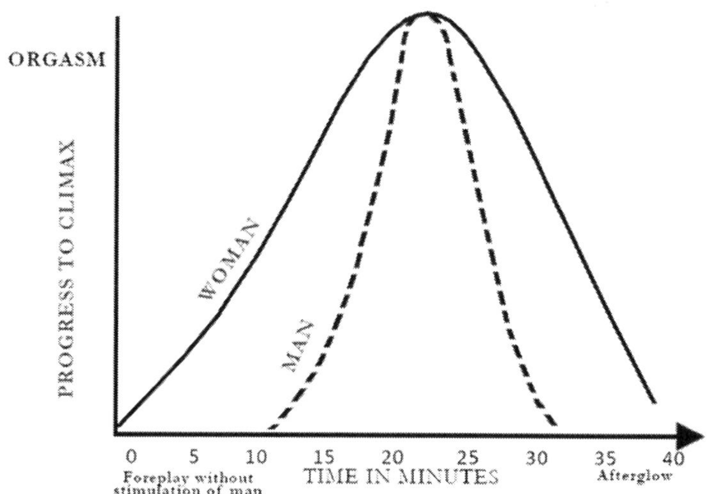

as he pursues his wife's satisfaction with foreplay until she is ready for intercourse. Even then he needs to allow her to determine how intercourse is to be conducted. If it is too vigorous or takes place too soon, it can be irritating and counterproductive to her progress. Caring consideration and listening to her needs will lead to the desirable goal of simultaneous orgasm.

SEXUAL TECHNIQUE

This brings us to a consideration of sexual technique as it pertains to intimacy. This final section is not an exhaustive discussion of sexual skills, but a specific look at the skills we need to conduct sexual intercourse in developing the fulfilment of intimacy.

To begin with, the art of loving caress or touch is important. We need to develop our ability to give pleasure through touch, from nonsexual touching to foreplay. Nonsexual but sensuous touch includes the gentle massaging of the feet or neck and tickling of the back, arms, legs and face. This should all happen with the attention focused on one another, through loving communication and concentration on giving pleasure and relaxing each other. It culminates in genital stimulation or sexual foreplay.

Another aspect of foreplay is kissing. There is an almost total involvement with one another sensually in the act of kissing. The senses of sight, hearing, touch, taste and smell are all engaged in enjoying one another. These combine to produce a build-up of sexual tension. The progression from kissing to other forms of direct sexual stimulation, is a natural and necessary one. Kissing is not only to be engaged in as a part of foreplay, but continued during and after intercourse. It maintains the totality of involvement necessary to intimacy during intercourse and is a beautiful means of enjoying the afterglow of intercourse.

Through the process of touching, caressing and kissing, women secrete lubricants for foreplay that make the manual stimulation of her genit<;tl organs pleasurable rather than painful. Husbands who lack consideration and rush foreplay can inflict pain and make intercourse itself painful. Intimacy, manifested in communication and a desire to please, will avoid the association of sex with pain, which is the precursor of many negative attitudes that women have to sex.

Foreplay at this stage is the gentle stimulation of especially the wife's genitalia, focusing on the clitoris, while she may stimulate her husband's genitalia provided that he is able to control his ejaculation until she is ready.

A woman knows when she is ready for intercourse. She must tell her husband when their foreplay has readied her for intercourse and the form it should take. Gentle, shallow and slow intercourse is usually preferable at the start, with a natural build-up to a more passionate style as the climax is approached. Thrusting that is too robust early on, can undo the good that has been done. Intimacy will have created the climate for intercourse to be conducted through open lines of communication. Selfish conduct during intercourse is a denial of true intimacy.

The duration of intercourse is also an important facilitator of intimacy. Trying to reach a climax in the shortest possible time is selfish and robs sex of its role of promoting intimacy. Ironically, quick sex also reduces the strength of orgasm for both partners. The longer intercourse lasts, the more satisfying the orgasmic release will be. Do you detect the moral in God's creative design of men and women?

UNUSUAL PRACTICES

I am sometimes asked in marriage counselling about the ethical and biblical admissibility of unusual practices in sex. This would include oral sex, anal intercourse, transvestitism and other fantasy methods of stimulation, and the use of mechanical means like vibrators. The Bible is often silent about specific questions, but it does uphold certain values in sexual practice. Let us look at the broad principles rather than try to address specific questions. The first principle that needs to govern our sexual behaviour is that intimacy must rule. Any practice that substitutes personal knowing with an impersonal means of stimulation violates this principle. This includes a practice that could be engaged in without your partner. One woman observed cynically: "Now that

I have an electric mower and a vibrator, who needs a man?" This reflects depersonalized sex that would be inimical to intimacy even if a man were present. A second principle is mutuality. Does the practice involve mutual enjoyment and satisfaction? Do both partners want to engage in it? Will it lead to mutual orgasm? This principle would usually rule out practices like anal intercourse. The third principle to guide sexual practice is exclusivity. The focus must be exclusively on my partner. I have referred to the destructiveness of fantasizing about sex with someone else. Playing games where a man can only be aroused if his wife dresses up like a schoolgirl or he dresses like a woman is a form of mental adultery or worse and is therefore a negation of this principle. It is also often indicative of serious confusion about sexual identity. I have said that homosexuality is a perversion. Any tendency towards homosexuality must be avoided if your sexual relationship is to be fulfilling. Transvestitism is such a tendency. A final principle is that all sex must foster mutual dignity. When a sexual practice demeans the personhood of either partner, this principle is violated. A practice that is demanded rather than spontaneously given involves a loss of personhood. When a partner has indicated that something is distasteful or causes her to lose her dignity, no loving partner will ever ask it of her. Discuss these principles together. If you agree with them, decide what they mean for your sexual practice. The issue for our marriages is not how I can become a sexual superstar, but how I can best please the unique, special person God has given me as a marriage partner and lover.

Your sexual love is meant to be a satisfying and growing dimension of your love throughout your marriage. Good lovers do not fade. They may mellow and they certainly become more relaxed in their loving as time passes, but cultivate your growth as a lover by reading healthy, valueorientated books on the subject such as those listed in the Sources. Be knowledgeable, develop your skills, refine your attitudes, and prepare for many powerful liftoffs and many fine landings.

And now that you have read the last chapter first, go back and read the others!

SOURCES

Abbey, Merrill R. Communication in Pulpit and Parish. Philadelphia: Westminster Press. 197 6.

Adams, Jay E. Christian Living in the Home. Grand Rapids:

Baker Book House. 1979.

Berne, Eric M.D. Games People Play. London: Penguin. 1964.

Bustanoby, Andr, S. Can Men and Women Be Just Friends? Grand Rapids: Zondervan Publishing House. 1985.

Encyclopaedia Britannica Macropaedia. Chicago: Helen Hemmingway Benton. 1974.

Grant, Toni. Being a Woman. New York: Random House. 1988. Hersey, Paul and Kenneth H. Blanchard. Management of Organizational Behavior. New Jersey: Prentice-Hall. 1977.

Harris, T.A. I'm O.K., You're O.K.. London: Jonathan Cape. 1973.

Kubler-Ross, Elizabeth. On Death and Dying. New York: Macmillan. 1969.

LaHaye, Tim and Beverly. The Act of Marriage: The Beauty of

Sexual Love. Grand Rapids: Zondervan Publishing House. 1976. Meyer, Paul J. Dynamics of Goal Setting. Waco: Success Motivation Institute, Inc .. 1983.

Penfield, Wilfred. "Memory Mechanisms". Archives of Neurology and Psychiatry, No. 67. 1952.

Penfield, Wilfred and H.H. Jasper. Epilepsy and the Functional Anatomy of the Human Brain. London: Churchill Press. 1954. Powell, John S.J. Why Am I Afraid to Tell You Who I Am? Allen: Tabor Publishing. 1969.

Pytches, Mary. Set My People Free. London: Hodder and Stoughton. 1987.

Rainey, Dennis. Lonely Husbands, Lonely Wives. Milton Keynes: Word (UK). 1990.

Made in United States
Orlando, FL
16 April 2023

32149782R00080